TEACH AND STILL HAVE TIME TO PEE

Jamie Johnson

Kickass Teacher

Copyright © 2020 Jamie Johnson

All rights reserved

No part of this book may be reproduced, or stored in a retrieval system, or transmitted in any form or by any means, electronic, mechanical, photocopying, recording, or otherwise, without express written permission of the publisher.

ISBN-13: 9798651555598

Cover design by: Jamie Johnson
Photo by: Pixaby
Printed in the United States of America

To the dedicated teachers, like my friend Judy Rasmussen, who need to be reminded how much their happiness and joy matters because it is the foundation of a great school.

Fear of realizing the dream ... is the most dangerous of obstacles because it has a kind of saintly aura about it: renouncing joy and conquest.

But if you believe yourself worthy, ... then you become an instrument of God, you help the Soul of the World, and you understand why you are here.

Know that the Universe is conspiring in our favor, even though we may not understand how.
— PAULO COELHO, THE ALCHEMIST

YOU ARE WORTH MORE THAN THE PILE ON YOUR DESK!

This book is for the teacher scrolling through open barista positions and crying over inspirational Facebook posts about other people quitting their jobs to go live the life of their dreams in Fiji. From a desk piled so high with unfinished work that there is no place to set her coffee, she sees other people; free, laughing, making a difference, and being celebrated for it and she wonders what could possibly be the first step to start her own journey to that magical island.

I'm talking to the teacher who is slowly falling apart from all of the kicking and screaming you do for your students and colleagues, only to hear "Who's gonna pay for that? That's just the way it is. Live with it!"

This book is for you! The dedicated, hardworking teacher putting everything into being kind, compassionate, and doing incredible teaching for your students. The amazing teacher who is rocking their work and is so tired and angry and demoralized from always having too much on your plate.

> *YOU ARE WORTH MORE THAN ANYTHING IN THAT PILE ON YOUR DESK!*

You are precious to our world and our students, young and old. Wise ones from ancient times have written about the importance of teachers. Of the four reliances in Buddhism, teaching is revered as the second most valued service to rely on even above one's own wisdom. The book of First Corinthians (12:28) states that teachers are placed third in the church, ahead of performing miracles and the gifts of healing.

You are a well-educated professional with a calling to improve lives, societies, culture, and generations! You hold a position to be heard, respected, and honored. You know your students and their needs better than any policy maker living across the nation who may have no background in teaching math or literacy. Trust the power of your learning, the power of your connection to real live students, your compassion, and your drive to make a difference. These are the things that will bring about world peace! Can you imagine if every single teacher was happy, healthy, and heard? The ripple of joy we could spread globally would result in nothing less than world peace! This book is my invitation for you to embrace your potential to bring about actual world peace. THAT MIRACLE CAN HAPPEN. Yes! YOU hold that power.

The first step to world peace is happy teachers. And the first step to happy teachers is any step that honors ourselves and this vessel that houses our spirit, heart, mind, and somatic system; this vessel we call our body. The receptacle that shows up every day to help, create, decide, move, shift, and TEACH! We are worth the commitment and effort it takes to stay energized, loved, and balanced. Because, when our bodies, minds, hearts, or spirits fail, we no longer have the energy to combat injustice, to create, nor to serve, which are all vital parts of this calling.

The mistake I used to make was powering through — Believing that if I wasn't the one to do it, it wouldn't get done — Believing I HAD to do everything that was mandated or plopped on my plate — Believing that pushing myself to get more done was the answer — Believing that if something/anything/everything wasn't done, I had failed in some way — Believing that it was a worthy endeavor to try to do everything everyone else expected of me.

I'm writing this to show you, you beautiful, powerful, worthy, bringer of knowledge and giver of choice, that you don't HAVE to do it all to be great! You do have a choice! I respect your knowledge, opinion, and wisdom. I want to hear your voice! I know that you already have everything it takes to be an amazing teacher, and even if you never take another training, class, or professional development course, you will still rock your teaching through to retirement.

This is permission to set down the overload of ideas you are carrying like bags of concrete piled on your back. This is permission to lighten your load, take a rest, and understand that you don't need any more new ideas. You already have that one perfect idea that will fulfill your desire to impact your students in profound ways. This is permission to replenish yourself first, set some courageous boundaries, and get the rest and inspiration you not only deserve, but NEED to continue shining your light in an environment that can, at times, be very dark.

We need you! We need your light! We need your inner beauty and your smiles. We need your knowledge and expertise. You ARE the positive difference in this world.

And so, my fellow world-shaper, I write this book to

be a cup-filler and inspiration to you. This book is a step toward honoring your holy vessel by showing you how to find some time to relieve your bladder and to enlist your spirit in bringing about world peace, through we, the teachers.

We are worth it!

Love,

Jamie J

PREFACE

I have been waiting and dreaming about writing a book to support teachers like the 25 year old version of myself — excited, hopeful, passionate. But, I didn't think I should attempt it until I had all the ideas just right and had life changing answers to all of life's questions. Well, the more I live and learn, the more I realize every moment brings new ideas, new answers, and I will never have them "all." Then along came a message…

"Just write your crappy book!" Wait..What?!! Are you saying my book doesn't have to be a world changing masterpiece? Interesting…maybe I can write a book!

This bit of wisdom came to me from a business coach who mostly showed me the kind of entrepreneur I never wanted to be and yet, he left me with a powerful gift; the reminder that no one needs me or my book to be perfect. No one expects me to have all of the answers. I decided I would let go of self-doubt and judgement to give writing a try.

So... welcome to my crappy book (pardon the bad pun).

This book is not for everyone. This book is for the teacher who hates their job and LOVES their work. The one who hates biased unjust systems and bureaucracies but LOVES teaching. If you feel there is nothing wrong with how teachers are treated, this book is not for you. If teaching doesn't include some sense of doing battle, this book is not for you.

This isn't a "chin up buttercup" kind of book. I'm not going to tell you to have grit and be resilient. I know that any teacher who has been in the classroom more than a minute already possesses those things and anyone who claims otherwise, doesn't know what it takes to walk through that door each morning.

I'm not here with "the answer." That particular holy grail doesn't exist. Only you have the answers that will work for you. I'm not here to "should" on you as in, "you should be doing this or should be doing that." The insights I share here are based on twenty years of discovery; filtered through the privileged lens and biases of a white American woman. My hope is that you will keep a copy near your favorite commode and read this in those small quiet moments to find one small nugget within one small section useful; something you connect with or can relate to that supports your own special you. Enjoy it, sit with it, relax with the ideas. Give yourself grace. Give yourself time to grow. That tiny nugget may have taken me five years to master. You're already ahead of the game just by knowing the change you want to make. No one knows better than you what you or your students need, so I invite you to use this book as a launch pad toward empowered teaching that aligns with your own values and practices. You got this!

YOU'RE ALREADY ENOUGH.

World hunger warrior, philanthropist, and adventurer, Lynne Twist, says in her book, The Soul of Money, "...Before we even sit up in bed, before our feet touch the floor, we're already inadequate, already behind, already losing, already lacking something. And by the time we go to bed at night, our minds are racing with a litany of what we didn't get, or didn't get done that day."

It pisses me off when people tell me to be present and stay mindful when my mind feels like it's on the hamster wheel of chaos. I have lessons to plan, papers to grade, parents to call — and to prove that

I am, in-fact, teaching, I have hours to spend preparing my own professional evaluation. How the heck do I stay present?

I always made sure to buy a plan book with a nice big blank section for me to list, "All of the things I have to do TODAY!" Checking off those boxes makes me feel like an A+++ Student. But, as each day comes to an end, I look at that list and suddenly can't breathe when I realize I'll have to stay at school until next February to get it all done (and that's just today's list). Eventually, I have to eat dinner, so I push those unfinished tasks back and now I'm already behind for tomorrow. Yikes! This pattern leaves me feeling defeated by the things I didn't get to, just as Twist said I would.

However, as another hero of mine, Byron Katie, states in her self-inquiry courses called *The Work*, "Everything we need to do can be done now."

Well, crap! I've been going about this all wrong and blindly following a strategy that leads me to believe I'm not enough. I have been stuck in a scarcity mindset and socially conditioned to accept it as truth.

The biggest mindset trap I stepped into was believing in the words "Have to." As in *I **have to** grade these papers. My boss says I **have to** turn in lesson plans on Monday. I **have to** write a different learning target on the board every day.* The truth is I don't even have to breathe if I don't want to.

My young cousin used to hold her breath until she passed out when she was angry. She realized (at two years old) that she had the power of choice over even the most basic function of her body. I personally WANT to breathe, I GET to breathe, I'm WILLING to breathe, I enjoy breathing, but it's a choice — a healthy choice that I want to make. Looking at the mandates, new curriculums, pressure from parents, administrators, society, and mostly myself, as something "I *have to* do," builds up anxiety, resentment, and panic within me. So the question is, *do I really have to do all of that?* Which leads to the questions, *what am I willing to do and what am I not willing to do? How do I decide what gets cut so I have time for a tinkle?*

I took a break down and leaving my job of ten years before I realized that it was time to change my mindset and step out of the mental trap of scarcity; believing I was always behind and not doing enough. Up until that point, I had been making a long unrealistic inventory of stuff I wanted to accomplish by the end of the day called my *To Do List* (maybe you've heard of it). It was loaded with things that I didn't need to write down and things that didn't actually need to be done that day: laundry, check email, grade math tests, input data, study Spanish, take down bulletin board, clean whiteboard, pick up groceries, organize library, clean keyboards, feed the crayfish, do the dishes, make dinner, make lunches, clean out purse, etc. Do I really need to write down a reminder to clean my purse or make dinner?

The To Do List is not the same as a calendar or reminder list. It's a catalog of things I don't actually need help remembering — things that if left undone, will not spoil the day. When something becomes urgent, I'll get on it. I will notice if I don't do my laundry for a month. I'll get to it when it's important but I don't need to write it down and then feel bad when I fail to get it done at the end of an exhausting day. If I don't grade my math tests today, I'll get to it when I need the data. I can trust myself to get to it without putting it on a list that beats me down every time I decide to put something off. If I'm honestly forgetting these kinds of things and become oblivious to a month's worth of laundry piled up, it's time for me to take a week's worth of mental health days and get some support, like a housekeeper, an life coach, or a therapist. Grossly neglecting the sacred space where I live, love, and sleep is a bright red flag waving wildly in my face telling me that I'm working way too hard and forgetting myself — a subconscious cry to set some courageous boundaries and get the rest and support I need and deserve.

Since I knew the *To Do List* was mental and emotional poison, I asked myself *What would be the opposite of that?* I imagined the opposite of the *To Do List* would be starting blank and adding to the list as I accomplish things throughout the day. Start with an empty cup and fill it up. That way maybe instead of feeling defeated by laundry that I didn't get crossed off the list, I can feel accomplished as I put it on my list of everything that got done — CHECK. I realized that I didn't need to think about the whole list of things to do. I only needed to to think about what could be done now.

I went cold turkey here and completely tossed my lists. I started by sitting down right then and making a list of the things I had already accomplished that day instead of lamenting the pending projects yet to be done. I called it my *Ta-Da List*.

After four days of practicing my new *Ta-Da List*, I woke up on a Saturday and saw the pile of dishes in the sink and didn't think, "Ugh. I have to do the dishes." Instead I thought with actual excitement, "Ooooh! Something I could add to my *Ta-Da List* today — if I decide to do them!" At that moment I realized I WANTED to do them rather than HAD to do them. There was a spare moment where I had six minutes in between client calls so I set my timer to get those dishes on my list of awesome accomplishments for today. Whatever I could get washed in six minutes would be enough. In those few minutes, I discovered it doesn't have to be perfect, or even complete, to be enough.

There were still some cucumber peels in the sink and a spoon I missed but I felt proud and relieved that the dishes were done enough for me to be happy and add them to my *Ta-Da List* for the day.

Realizing that, for something to be celebrated on my Ta-Da List, it didn't have to be completely finished was like that first day you can throw open your windows in the spring time after a long winter. In my scarcity mindset, it didn't count unless it was DONE. Then I realized that with a mindset focused on *enough*, whatever and however I get something done, it counts and is definitely worth celebrating. So my bulletin board is missing the bottom boarder. I'm celebrating that I got something up. I have six of 23 report cards done. I get to celebrate the six.

As a teacher, I, of course, love to give myself stickers on the calendar to honor my hard work and attempts at well-being. I found some "Adulting" stickers that say things like, "I shaved my legs," "Folded my laundry," and "Washed my hair today." My Ta-Da List includes the accomplishments I make toward not only work, but also refreshing my space, taking care of my body, uplifting my spirit, and other intentional well-being practices which research has shown to improve motivation and productivity. I get a star for things like: going for a walk to get coffee at recess, taking a nap at lunch, going out for lunch, taking my whole break, and of course making it to the bathroom. Every time I do the particular self-care activity I'm focusing on for the month, I get a sticker for that day. It can be as simple as drinking a glass of water...not a gallon, not five glasses, just ONE. I also get one for accomplishing my ONE big goal for the day (that's not code for twenty things rolled into one). Grade math tests could be my one goal and that's all I focus on for the day. I don't add anything else to my goal for the day.

Wait, so how is a goal different from a To Do List?

There are things I do need help remembering. I don't have the birthdays of all my friends memorized any better than I remember when our next IEP meeting will be. I do keep an "Idea list" of things I refer to when I'm looking for ideas to add to my Ta-Da List, and I keep important events and due dates in my planner. I create a map for my month with ONE overarching target and then create a weekly map doing the same. The key is to have ONE thing to focus on and outline how I can get there. This is tricky with thirteen subjects to teach at seven different grade levels. My focus for the week may be science. I'm still going to teach math but my energy and best lessons will be in science. I know it means taking a deep breath and accepting the truth that whatever I get done is enough, my students are enough, and I am enough.

The big difference is that I no longer create a daily list of what I **have to** get done. I trust I'll know what is most important for me to work on right now. Once I started doing this full time, I noticed how that old to-do list of mostly failures had been sucking away my self-efficacy and motivation.

You don't have to jump in cold turkey like I did. It can be scary trusting your memory and the moment to carry you where you need to go. I recommend starting by setting aside your To Do List. Sit down with your favorite color pen or pencil and some beautiful paper or a pleasant list app on your phone, smile, exhale, and start listing every little tiny thing you have done today. Remember to include love and relationships. Did you talk to your mother on the phone? Did you listen to something inspirational? Did you get outside and breathe some fresh air? Those things count just as much as inputting data and going to meetings. List until you can't list anymore. Now compare your lists. Now celebrate. Notice how much you totally rock! How much longer is your *Ta-Da List*? How do you feel? (Seriously! Email me, I'd love to know)!

Now that you have that part down, look at your current *To Do List* and notice all of the things on there that you really don't need help remembering. Stop writing those down as *To Do* and start leaving space to wave your magic wand and celebrate them as Ta-Da, done. I only record appointments and my one big goal for the day in my planner now. The rest gets filled up as I go.

Making this shift from worrying about what *has to get done* to focusing on what I have already accomplished each day has rejuvenated my motivation. Instead of leaving hopeless at the end of the day, I celebrate how productive and healthy my day was and I honor the dedicated person I am and the wholehearted life I'm living. My list of accomplishments is far longer than my To Do List ever was and I feel grounded in my sense of purpose. Letting go of the mountain of minutia gave me that vital time to powder my nose.

If you read no further and this is THE nugget you take away from this book, it is ENOUGH! If you take nothing else away, take this affirmation as my gift to you.

I do enough, I have enough, and I am enough.

MAKING SPACE FOR JOY

My lifelong dream of living in a developing world abroad was about to come true. I felt like I was standing in one those exotic photos from my traveling heroes, about to embark on my own new adventure; my teaching gig in a remote village of Indonesia. When I finally saw the school and realized we had whiteboards I was thrilled! I had been in classrooms in India and Ghana that were open air under a tree, so to have a school with tables and whiteboards opened up a whole new realm of possibilities for us. Then, I noticed there were no markers to go with the whiteboards....

Luckily, I had been honing my resourcefulness and focusing on minimalist teaching practices long before Peace Corps. Being resourceful is a quality I have always admired. A person who is resourceful can go beyond surviving to thriving in a pure and simple existence. When it comes to my teaching and my life, less is more. When I say less, I'm talking about time, money, paper, furniture, ideas, rules, doing, clutter, outdated materials, things, and options in general. I mean aggressively simplifying things down to only the highly valuable core; leaving as much open space on the walls, on the floor, on the shelves, and in our minds as possible. Open space is restful. Open space unfolds the mind so new knowledge can enter.

SAVE THE TREES AND SAVE YOUR WEEKENDS

The first thing I pruned to create more temporal open space was the never ending task of making copies. I wasted hours at the copy machine and was not modeling good Earth stewardship by going through reams of unnecessary paper each day. What was the point of all of those copies?

When I was in middle school, I remember the joy of stuffing piles of old homework into the fireplace and watching it burn. Worksheets had no staying power and no personal meaning to me. I was glad school was over and I didn't have to fill in the blanks anymore. So, once I became a teacher, I remembered what a waste of time those papers had been. Even though a lot of work is now done in digital format, the waste is the same. We ripped up and shredded old homework packets to make recycled paper as a class project. I know that the more personally meaningful learning is, the more it hits home. So, I made it a game to see how few copies I could get away with and soon found I could easily go a week without making any.

I started asking what was truly worth standing at the machine and sacrificing trees for? Anything published by my third graders that could be shared with the class was unquestionably worth time at the machine to me. We would create take-home class books that were a collection of student created math story problems with pictures, poetry, or short stories so students could celebrate their own work and build an at-home library. I noticed most of my worksheets and student workbooks had too many questions and were overly wordy to really get to the heart of the lesson (especially for my students new to English). I decided to cut that down by selecting one or two key questions or items from a worksheet to dig into and if necessary, would have students copy the prompt, outline, or template from the board into their journal themselves. Learning to copy from the board was challenging for some, especially in primary grades, and I knew it was a skill many were missing but, once mastered, would serve them throughout the rest of their educational career.

I also had my classes chronicle their learning adventures each year in a student learning journal. There were a few copied lessons glued in here and there but for the most part their journal was in their own hand. This looks different at the primary grades with more drawing and a few short sentences but this still means a lot to the student creating it. Remember, you know best what will work for your students and your teaching style. Journals are one way that worked really well for me from the third to high school levels and how that would work for you is up to your preference, expertise and creativity. I knew students would learn more from one hand drawn graph than from ten photocopied graphs that they filled in or tapped on their tablet.

By cutting out the copies, we spent much more time learning by "doing" and much less time mindlessly filling in empty blanks in workbooks or tapping on screens. I spent less time producing work for the students to do and more time asking them important questions. That meant I had to learn to trust myself by letting go of the conditioning within a system that had convinced me (the teacher) that I was not knowledgeable or educated enough to step out of the script. I slowed things down. Instead of a math test with 40 questions, I would create a couple of math tests with ONE well-crafted question to demonstrate individual progress. This saved time grading and created more space for learning rather than testing. It brought down the blood pressure for us all and made it much easier to determine who needed what next. I finally had the one on one time to build stronger relationships with my students and get to know them better.

By pruning down the extra paper, my grading became much simpler and clearer for students and parents to understand. One concept at a time with clear evidence of which students "got it" or "don't got it," as one of my favorite colleagues used to say, is all my students and I need to understand the next step and when to tackle it. I also assigned minimal homework and even tried to get rid of homework all together once I discovered how ineffective it had been shown it to be by current research. The parents rioted and demanded homework so, in the end, I compromised by digging back into the research to find out which types of homework were most useful and assigning only those. Handwriting practice, reading books (which was never off the table), and math facts practice. Getting out from under the piles of paper and content creation provided me more space to enjoy my dinner time and hot dates with myself or someone special on the weekends!

I realized that I was the one creating a ton of extra work for myself by giving too many assignments and trying to fit too much into one lesson. I don't have to exhaust myself nor my students by overworking all of us. My first step to making this happen, was to find a way to use less paper and slow down the learning enough to do more in the student's own hand.

WALLS OF CHAOS TO A SANCTUARY OF CALM

Another example of pruning down the garden of my classroom involves one of my biggest pet peeves — *sensory overload*. I can't stand walking into a room with every inch of every wall covered in every color of the rainbow about every topic we will cover for the entire year. If I get a headache from the visual overload as a teacher without learning issues, what does this do to my students with learning difficulties, distractibility, dyslexia, and/or language barriers? My goal was to be intensely selective about the few key items I put up at a time, leaving more comfortable, peaceful, open space for the mind to clear and rest. I feel calmer not having every inch of my walls serve as a reminder of the teaching I haven't gotten to or everything my students haven't fully grasped. When my walls are not one big piled up "to do list" for me and my students, we can be more present with what we are discovering in the moment.

So where do I put all of that stuff that was on the walls? Some still provides that kick of joy as I toss it on the fire while a few carefully considered items make it into students' learning journals. Instead of the confusing chaos of cluttered walls, we'd refer back to things like daily learning targets and maps in our learning journals as needed. I taped small sticky note sized reminders to the own students' desks rather than have them on the wall. My bulletin boards became a dedicated space to celebrate student work and keep track of daily helpers. Of course, I needed to leave room for a few mandated items on the walls, and I liked to include one nature tapestry to relax into near the books. My quest was to keep our walls and minds peaceful so that when I walked into my classroom, it was like that moment I walk into a nature spa and breathe a deep relaxing sigh.

The less time I spent on the ladder putting up posters, the more time I had to enjoy lunch at my favorite little bistro down the street. Yes! I left the building to eat lunch. Teachers deserve every minute of our lunch time to be spent in peace! And, I knew that I couldn't count on someone else to hand me those minutes. I had to chisel them out of the granite face of what often felt like downright exploitation of kind people with a calling to serve.

SAVE YOUR MONEY AND SAVE YOUR JOY

Becoming resourceful with money and minimizing

my spending created space for plane tickets, hotel stays, fancy dinners, and my very own hot tub; a whole new world of options in my pursuit of well-being. I started out spending about $4,000 of my $27K salary each year in my classroom. The overspending on my classroom led to sacrificing trips to Hawaii, tuition for my continuing education and it increased the emotional stress of trying to pay my bills on such a meager salary. Essentially, it was wreaking havoc on my overall peace of mind. It wasn't long before I realized how much I needed those trips to the beach to preserve my sanity and mental clarity. I quit spending **any** of my own money and even with a zero dollar budget, I still won tech awards and teacher of the month for our small city because I learned to look for grants and ASK FOR WHAT I NEED.

One brand-new teacher recently asked what I wish I had known to stock up on for my first classroom.

I replied:

> *I wish I had known that our school had a centralized location for class supplies. I bought a bunch of stuff I didn't know the school already provided. I should have filled out a purchase order for EVERYTHING first and only bought the stuff my principal rejected (which she rarely did). I wish I had known that I could take most of the required student supplies (at my 91% poverty school) off the list and have*

the school purchase Ticonderoga pencils, scissors, erasers, and highlighters, etc., to save families the extra financial stress. I wish I had known to ask for what I needed at the start. I mastered THE ASK in the end and made a point of sharing my secrets with as many teachers as I could. And here I am, sharing them with you!

It's ok to ask for what you need. You deserve support. Ask and ask until you find your tribe; the people who are thrilled to help.

Another great trick up my sleeve was keeping a wish list ready for those rare occasions when $300 would suddenly be available but only if spent within 24 hours. I learned to look for grants and enter contests for class prizes. I learned to make the most of my Scholastic book club's free and $1 books (they make great Christmas presents). I learned to ask parents for snacks and ended up with teachers and community members contributing as well. I learned that you can get a month's worth of pretzels at Costco for $5, and that, with a little ingenuity, Cheerios can go a long way. Most of all, I learned that if I don't already have it, I probably don't really need it. I shifted from focusing on scarcity to seeing enough!

Eliminating my own spending in class did so much more than pay for my plane tickets to exotic beaches. It taught me to see the core of what was important in achieving student learning and to stop chasing ten-thousand ideas. It kept me from overloading my students and myself with too many questions, too much homework, and an overly complicated lesson or classroom environment. It created more space for building relationships with my students and to become an expert on the few teaching materials I held most precious. Instead of spending more money on other people's ideas, I began to trust my own expertise. I trusted myself to discern my students' needs better than anyone; better than anyone at Teachers Pay Teachers or even in the White House. I began to recognize myself as a well-educated and dedicated professional. Some viewed my lack of spending as selfish, but when I stopped using my own limited income to supplement my classroom I became more resourceful; a teacher who no longer bought her lessons and perfect classroom at the expense of her own health and happiness but who now worked with students to create a simple and personally meaningful space to learn and celebrate students and the mindset that we are already enough, have enough, and do enough.

So, what did I do about the whiteboard with no markers?
I bought some stinking markers! But finding them took months and, during the search, the lack of those markers created space for me to expand my resourcefulness and creativity on a whole new level. Learning to see that I already had enough, created

monetary space for me to take those trips to Paris and spend a little on a massage. Drawing a hard line and setting courageous boundaries around my joy and my values, brings that joy right back into my work and that's how I know happy teachers have the power to bring about world peace!

A FRESH CUT

Zzzzip, zzzzzip, zzzzzzip. That's the satisfying sound of scissors sliding though plastic lamination as I made hundreds of cuts trying to get posters ready for the wall tomorrow. It was 9:00 PM, and I hadn't had dinner, or lunch for that matter. I jumped out of my skin when, Jack, the custodian popped into the work room to tell me that he would be leaving soon and needed to set the alarms. Shoot! I was only about halfway through my project!

Is this why I worked my ass off for a Master's degree; to be up all night cutting laminating? I thought sarcastically to myself. Then, through that cloud of frustration, a light turned on in my head. *What the EFF am I DOING?!!* I haven't eaten. I'm not getting enough sleep. I never get outside. I'm wasting my life doing things like cutting this laminating! This is a task that is not worth giving up my health and happiness for. This can be done by ANYONE. I don't need a degree to cut out posters. I wrapped up what was left and set it on the desk of my "helper of the day" for tomorrow. She was thrilled to be given this task. From then on, my students cut their own laminating and, at first, it wasn't pretty but even pretty laminating isn't worth giving up that potty precious!

I removed the blinders I'd been wearing that made me believe in the words "***have to***" *and* noticed that the pile on my desk was full of tasks that didn't take a master's degree to complete. I sorted that mountain of **to do** into three piles. Pile ONE held things that anyone could do; things that took almost no skill or training like: cutting laminating, stapling books, passing back papers and journals, filing the lunch cards, organizing a box of books.

Pile TWO consisted of things that took some knowledge or skill to complete but volunteers, parents, and friends could easily accomplish, such as: binding A-Z books, grading multiple choice test questions, data entry, cleaning the crayfish tank, rotating the helper of the day cards, loading new audio books onto the iPods.

At that point, these two piles no longer lived on my desk. I detached myself from them by putting them in boxes on a counter across the room. With both of these piles, I had to let go of my perfectionism and attachment to how it will look or what people will think in order to let someone else do the job in their own way. If the stapling was wonky or the handwriting wasn't perfect, I let go of my perfectionistic expectations and accepted the result without criticism or further direction so the one who did the work could take pride in their accomplishments and sense my deep gratitude.

Letting go of perfectionism is one of those difficult journeys that usually goes better with a guide like a strong role model, life coach, or therapist, any of which we teachers absolutely deserve to treat ourselves to and, better yet, be treated to. This kind of mindset shift doesn't happen overnight. It takes practice, commitment, and study. Like with the Ta-Da List, I learned to let go of perfect cuts and corners and completeness in my mind to clear away the mental space to celebrate each accomplishment as enough and worthy.

Pile THREE was exclusively reserved for the things that could ONLY be done by me. When I decided something could only be done by me it had to meet certain criteria: top-secret information was involved, my degrees and expertise were necessary to do it well, and it wasn't in the pile just because I wanted it done my way. This pile included things like: complex grading, district reports, grants to write, lesson planning, and correspondence.

The "only me" pile was my daily focus and the other two boxes could just sit there ready for when students came to me and said, "can I help?" Or, when the occasional para or volunteer with extra time would ask if I needed help. I always had something ready to hand over or send home with willing parents. And shit finally got done! It was amazing.

There were unexpected benefits of sharing the work load besides more time for eating, peeing, and enjoying life. With that first roll of laminating, my 4th grade students were ecstatic to have the chance to slice through such a wonderful substance as shiny clear plastic. Over time, they perfected that "zzzzzzip, zzzzzip" cutting and were empowered by new skills that developed more student independence. The more I handed them, the more involved they felt in their own education. Parents who didn't have time during the school day to help out, were excited to have things to staple or put together for me at home and I couldn't keep up with the increased demand from people I had previously thought were uninterested in school. New relationships were developed. Student self-efficacy increased, and I had a bit more time to breathe.

You are the only one who truly knows what goes in your three piles and what kind of things the other twenty-five pairs of hands in the room can do. I encourage you to give students a chance to surprise you. Let it "not go well" a few times until they get it. Imperfection is perfect when it creates time to enjoy peace and quiet in the bathroom.

The empowering mindset shift I embraced was — *I am human. I will no longer worship pain and martyrdom. I don't have to do it all myself. I'm not willing to beat myself up trying.* It takes a village to raise a child and I'm ready, willing, and actively building relationships and creating opportunities to include everyone in my village. I went from trying to do it all to allocating a villages worth of tasks. Making this clean cut is where I first realized that I am worth more than the pile on my desk! And, when I LIVE like I'm worth more than that pile, everyone around me benefits. They are worth more than that pile too.

SALTY NUTS

"Would you like to taste my nuts? They're salty." The father of one of my students smugly sank back into his recliner, lord of the manor style, as he offered me one of the most gut-wrenching insults imaginable in front of my precious and impressionable student.

When I moved up to 4th grade from 3rd, I miraculously convinced my two colleagues to start doing home visits for all of our students. I still can't believe they were crazy enough to agree with some of the ideas I proposed, but there we were, 9:00 at night, driving through lawns that we thought were parking lots and spinning in circles trying to find homes that were sometimes no more than sheds. There were many amazing and just a few sketchy moments. The best ended in laughter so hard it went silent because we couldn't breathe. We agreed at the start to never go alone and that these visits were not "checkups" but solely to build relationships and encourage our students' families, this is one of the best parts of teaching that gets left out. Each fall we would get together to hand-make funny little gifts to give students' families when we visited. I agreed to accompany my colleagues who needed my Spanish interpreting skills, which doubled my list of home visits but was worth it to experience a unified sense of purpose for something deeply meaningful to each of us.

I was down to the last lingering visit for the year and was having difficulty finding a time we could all agree on. The desire to be finished, as well as the thought that my student was starting to feel left out, convinced me I would be fine conducting the visit on my own. It was going well. My student was showing me his Legos and expressing overall amazement and joy that his teacher was in his home taking a genuine interest in his toys and accomplishments.

I was letting go of the pile on my desk and trading it to build the relationship and trust that makes teaching and learning happen faster, easier and more meaningfully. *Learning is vulnerable and full of risks. I don't take risks with people I don't trust and neither will my students.*

As that hardened and skeptical father reclined in his chair offering me his "salty nuts", I was so excited about the connection I was making with my student that I missed the innuendo and was popping some salty pistachios into my mouth before I noticed the horrified look on my student's face. I knew in that instant, as my mouth went dry and those pistachios turned to ash, that the father saw my intentions were sincere and his son was hurt by his cruelty. I could see his smug look turn to shame.

I said a quick and stiff goodbye, and went straight to my car to scream and rage and cry the molten lava hot tears of anger, insult, and heartbreak. I have often called the work I do with families "cracking nuts" in reference to the hard shells created around a heart by things like abusive school experiences and teachers who use shame to keep students in line. Many of my students' families suffered from horrible school experiences, so they assumed all schools or teachers were the same. I know that I have to crack through that nutshell, and once I do, I find the hope and the light that is buried there.

What does this have to do with surviving the teaching profession? PARENTS!

Parents and significant adults have the power, directly or vicariously, to make or break the year for a student and the teacher. I recently conducted a poll asking hundreds of teachers what the most painful part of teaching was. They overwhelmingly identified parents as the number one source of pain. Insulting, threatening, or disrespectful behavior and lack of support were the main issues.

This guy was not my first "salty nut' nor my last. I had parents coming to meetings high or drunk, hiding from me after I drove out to meet them at their workplace, and not showing up after I waited for them at school until 8PM. I heard parents tell their children that they don't have to do anything the teachers say (which I agree with, in a way, since I let go of **have to,** but I'll talk more about that later). I had parents who refused to talk to me while sitting at the same table, and parents who insulted and belittled me. I had parents who were active criminals (gunrunners and drug dealers) but worst of all were the parents who were harmful to their children. Despite all of that, I had to believe that I could get through to some significant adult in each child's life, and I've always found a way, even if it meant I had to let go of worrying about math tests for a while. I have many more stories of the swamps I've had to wade through to win parents over, but trudging through those swamps was easier in the end than continually being attacked, shunned, or disrespected. Without parents on my side, it was like bushwhacking through the jungle trying to reach their children. With engaged parents, it was like I had a nice clear path to the beach!

So how do I get parents who range from hardened criminals to wealthy lawyers to support and respect me as a teacher? How do I get them on my team?

To get all parents regardless of income level, culture,

or background to come to events, there are three things teachers and schools need to include:

1 Food

2 Help accessing free resources

3 A chance to watch their children perform

I'll share some of the ways that I used these in my classrooms and encourage you to remember that only you can determine what version of these three elements will work for you and your students without letting it become something extra added to your plate.

I discovered the *magic three* while working on my master's thesis, and once I started using them in my classroom, open houses became standing room only and I would have to shoo people out the door so they would go visit the other classrooms! For ten straight years I had 100% attendance at parent teacher conferences in a title I school with a poverty demographic always ranging in the low 90th percentile. By getting parents in the room to start with, I no longer had to waste time chasing people down. And, because they saw that it was the norm to show up, it became easier and easier to get people into the classroom, event after event, and year after year. Again, I'd rather take a path to the beach than bushwhack through the jungle, even if it means I have to spend some time cleaning that path in the beginning.

Here's a bit about how I interpreted and implemented these 3 magical reluctant-parent-magnets!

FOOD

Food is one of our basic needs, and when I'm meeting those needs, I help people step out of their "fear brain" and into a relaxed cerebral cortex, ready to learn and converse. I didn't have to host a catered event in my room to attract families; less can be more in this case (especially with cleanup).

One year, I had a jar of M&M's and the family who guessed closest to the number in the jar would win the whole jar. This simple bit of food being offered was so successful that when I finished my standing-room only presentation, I was left awkwardly saying, "That's it. Did I forget something? What are you all still here for?" One parent raised her hand and said, "Who won the jar?" We all laughed at the relief from such suspense as I sorted out who won the M&M's. The more parents I get in the room for one large meeting, the less time I spend explaining the same things over and over again one on one.

You know best what your families will love and what is available when it comes to making food a part of your events. Some teachers may have parents who would be happy to take on the food preparation and clean up role for an open house. Ooooh, I haven't tried this yet but what if a local restaurant was willing to donate something for your class! I recently saw a social media post about a school that invited a food truck to park in the lot for the day and the administration gave all of the teachers $10 to spend at lunch. This could work for an open house night for students and families as well. Get creative and make sure it's not simply more on your plate. Ask the whole village to help.

PROVIDING ACCESS TO RESOURCES

To include access to resources, I studied research on building the school-home relationships for my specific student demographics. On the surface, many of my students' parents appeared to be unsupportive but underneath it all they truly wanted to see their child succeed in school. I knew that oftentimes a phone call or filling out a form was the only thing stopping my non-English speaking parents from having access to powerful resources. During conferences, I would invite the local librarian to come hang out in our hallway and help parents get library access for their family. My principal, other teachers, and our counselor came on board with this as well and we invited many different people to help provide support filling out paperwork and answering questions about healthcare/insurance or other community services. Seeing people get what they need for FREE, feeds my Libra nature's desire to see balance and justice in the world. Getting valuable resources into the homes of my students gave me a more powerful sense of purpose than anything in the pile on my desk. Time spent on these kinds of resources is benefited me and my student far more than the time I had been spending on fighting to get homework turned in on time or at all.

This was one area I spent a lot of time bushwhacking my own path to that magical beach until other staff saw the impact these kinds of resources were having on student performance. Once I got it started, our family advocate, instructional coaches, and community members started to take over most of these tasks and I ended up with even more time to laugh with my favorite Far side comics in the bathroom!

A CHANCE TO SEE THEIR CHILDREN PERFORM

Including student performance took on many different forms. I had talent shows, videos, artwork, re-

corded reading and many other ways for families to simply see their children and what they could do. One favorite performance was my 3rd grade class "Coffee House." It was entirely student led and we dedicated a whole day to the show. Students ended up soliciting the support of the music teacher and other people outside of the classroom to put together anything they wanted to show.
There were wildly energetic dance offs, shy musical performances, poetry, short skits, and riotous stand up comedy. You could see the sense of accomplishment and pride the students had with the extra skip in their steps and uncontrollable smiles as they completed their grand works of art.

We had two different showing times, and not only did parents come, other teachers showed up during their prep time to see the kids shine. Did you catch that? DURING THEIR PREP TIME! They didn't have time to pee but they still came to watch their old students perform! I was amazed at what the students could do once I relinquished control and handed them over one of the most impactful pillars of human motivation; autonomy! I was also convinced this was the way to get more out of our year together with less of me dragging students down the street toward learning goals because of the affect ONE good performance had on the adults in my students' lives. We were all instantly a team for EVERYTHING.

Yes, I gave up some core curriculum time to work on

this. Yes, I probably blew off a mandate or two. During this year of COVID, we are seeing more clearly than ever the importance of putting Maslow before Bloom's; basic needs before learning targets. There's no point in trying to teach a math lesson if my students don't feel safe and cared for. Brains aren't even open to learning math until safety and trust are firmly established. Being adored by their parents and teachers was a great way to bring that safety and trust into my classroom.

GETTING PARENTS ON YOUR TEAM

Once I had used the magical three elements to get parents in the door for events, the next step was to get them on my team. One of the best moves my principal made was dumping the required weekly lesson plans and asking instead for monthly positive-parent-contact reports. At first, I thought this was just more in that pile on my desk but I decided an extra monthly task was better than an extra weekly task. And then I started making those calls to each family, sending home notes and newsletters, or meeting face-to-face with parents to share something positive about their child. This shifted both myself and the students' caregivers out of the fear-based mindset around all of the things that needed correcting for my students and into an assets based mindset that celebrated the strengths we all had to offer. Parents were no longer thinking, *uh-oh a call from the teacher. What is she going to complain about now?* And, I wasn't whining in my head, *Sheesh, I don't want to hear her yell at me about her son's missing homework. She hates talking to me.* We shifted into a mindset that celebrated *assets*. My students were all progressing at something worthwhile and worth sharing.

I noticed that the more I shared positive feedback and growth with angry and reluctant parents, the more they let go of their old beliefs about school and teachers being punitive and risky. We stepped into a partnership. I could share what their child was working on and one or two ways they could provide support at home. I made sure only to include things I thought the family could handle and that would quickly and easily show a positive result.

Some examples include: reading an easy and interesting book, practicing complimenting their siblings and family members, learning to subtract three from any number under twenty, count by three with Cheerios at home, the manner of the week, writing descending letters that drop below the line, getting outside and collecting as many leaf colors as they could find (for students with too much screen time), practicing a polite tone of voice even when frustrated, choosing books from our mail order library catalog and practicing filling out the form to order them (I would check and mail these for the students which saved me time choosing books and getting them to read at home). It could be anything I thought the student could do without much parental guidance and that the parent could easily monitor. Anything I could get families to support at home, cleared a path to accomplishing learning goals more quickly.

Families and I looked forward to talking to each other and they were much more receptive to difficult conversations when they came up. Talk about metaphorically clearing a path to some exotic beach! This move absolutely made my life easier and was far more effective in improving student performance than taking time to submit weekly lesson plans had been. Relationship matters more than anything and you know your business when it comes to teaching. No one but you needs weekly copies of your damn lesson plans. If you need support you deserve the space to ask for it as needed and direct what that support should look like. So, instead of putting energy into micromanaging lessons and test scores, you deserve leaders who are prepared to help you build healthy relationships within your school.

One of the most powerful shifts I encountered using this strategy was with a Native American family who, at first, would not speak one word to me (even when I was sitting right in front of them) but then over many meetings began to share vulnerable stories of the most horrific abuse and injustices based on the worst kind of prejudice and fear in this same school district over several generations. They helped me to understand why they were reluctant to give me a chance in a way that was both eye-opening as a woman of candy-coated-white-privilege and heart-wrenching as a person passionate about learning. The moment I hold most dear was a conversation on the phone with Grandmother who told me that her family felt old prejudices were finally leaving the school system and that they could trust their child would be cared for and well educated with us. Somehow this family still found it in their hearts to give the local public education system another chance. I am honored to have been welcomed into many families such as this and given a new chance to help their children make the exceptional academic and emotional growth they deserve.

A strong family connection not only saves time and energy in the classroom, but it creates a deeper sense of purpose and meaning in our work. Meaningful connections with colleagues and students are key to battling teacher demoralization. Building these positive relationships may seem like more on my plate but what I've learned is that I was allowing the wrong things to land on my plate in the first place. Relationships come first and everything else can wait.

Two days after the "Salty Nuts" incident, that same father came to my room and apologized. His demeanor was shockingly different, actually remorseful. From that day forward, when it came to helping his son achieve great things, I had his support.

This could have gone very differently. I could have made the mistake of going to this home visit thinking that this guy is a misogynistic ass who doesn't really give a shit about his child. I probably would have gone in "on guard" and caught his "salty nuts" innuendo right away. I would have given him the "Teacher eye" and left him feeling glad to have pissed off another know-it-all teacher who only wanted to humiliate his son, but I would still have been brokenhearted. Fortunately, I went in knowing, from ten years of experience with these kinds of "salty nuts," that he was a parent doing the best he could with what he had, and I trusted that he absolutely cared about his child and had his boy's best interest at heart. I was not on guard and the father saw that. He saw that I came with a sincere appreciation for his child and respect for him as a parent. He finally saw that we were teammates on a quest to support a young human who was important to us both.

I'm not suggesting that you miraculously find more time for the "john" by jumping into doing home visits. If you do, you will have some courageous cuts to create the space and time in your schedule. But I know connection matters more than anything. Building a relationship with your students that involves more than academics and progress, is the heart of happy teaching. Your relationships are worth more than test scores.

Relationships bring the sense of purpose we teachers crave. THAT is "the calling." Relationship make our work meaningful and worth standing up for by setting courageous boundaries that leave room for what's important to our hearts.

SWEARING IN SCHOOL

Who is this kick-ass teacher and why is she swearing in school?

I'm the girl who smuggles a kitten home from her Peace Corps village on the other side of the planet. I'm the one who sees a frail old woman struggling at the side of a river bank in Indonesia and runs to the rescue, only to discover she has gone there to pee. One time my curiosity almost killed me wondering what the heck a vagina massage could possibly be in a place where it was common knowledge that using a tampon could put your virginity at risk, and so, I dove into that adventure too.

I identify as a white, cisgender, Christian, American woman and that comes with a lot of privilege, especially when it comes to taking risks and making mistakes. Things that I'm able to laugh off could lead to catastrophe for a Black Indigenous Person of Color in the same situation. You know best which risks will empower your career and I encourage you to use my example as an imperfect starting point, or ending point, or not at all for that matter.

A short time ago, I was speaking in front of my largest audience of educators yet. It went so well that I was doing the happy dance in the bathroom afterward, and as I congratulated myself in the wall-wide mirror... I realized I had just spent an hour and a half teaching the keys to human motivation with my dress ripped down the seam, from armpit to waist. Boy was I glad I had on a pretty blue lacy bra that day! I can't even write this without cracking up.

I'm the girl that shares her most embarrassing moments with friends and they say, "Wow! We all talk about our embarrassing moments but YOURS are next level." Their laughter and amazement can leave me with no other reaction to myself and my faux pas, then to join them in their laughter, rolling on the ground and completely out of breath. When is the last time you laughed so hard you couldn't stand up? In laugher, there is no room for fear, shame, or regret. These times, laughing with friends, soothes the burn of humiliation and reveals the courage I need to embrace leaps of faith and believe in miracles.

What about the times when there is no room to laugh; when I'm ashamed because I was just plain wrong? How do I recover from that? First, I recognize that while I did something wrong, I'm not a bad person. Then I apologize as quickly as possible and clean up my mess. My biggest apologies have been the most powerful lessons on my quest to live an authentic life of integrity and unlimited adventure.

Being wrong hurts, the way leg cramps do when we stretch and grow. There are a few red flags that flap right in my face to warn me I have made a mistake. When I start making excuses, blaming, and feeling defensive I know it's time to exhale and look in the mirror. I disarm my defensiveness by looking honestly at how I contributed to the problem and admitting out loud that I was wrong, even if it's only to myself in the moment. It sounds so scary up until the point that I do it, and then, I feel the universe begin to swing back into balance and I move on. My fear of being wrong and making a mistake dissolves because I said it out loud and faced it — literally in the mirror — and it wasn't as bad as I had imagined (though that doesn't stop me from continuing to imagine the worst the next time). I keep proving to myself that facing my error before even trying to fix it works and is not that bad. It gets easier and easier, but slowly. Consistency is key and it's never too late to say *I was wrong*.

So, to survive teaching and still have time to pee, I let go of the pressure to be perfect, because chasing perfection is trudging along the path of someone else's standards. I've found the miracle of imperfection and enrolled in the university of screwing up because I've decided I like being human. I like a good laugh and a good story. I want to be a good model of resilience and growth. I can't pull that off without swinging a few wrecking balls!

Mistakes and imperfection are what have added color and closeness to my relationships with students, colleagues, and loved ones. A teacher who makes mistakes and celebrates students for catching her errors is a loved teacher. I love to watch my students become comfortable enough in class to point out things I forgot or got wrong. I love to see them realize that my self-worth is not diminished by being wrong and neither should theirs be. I love seeing them learn that they are part of an imperfect team and that we all deserve to be loved, as glitchy as we may be. I don't recommend speaking in front of a large audience with your zipper down (yep, I've done that too) but I DO recommend exposing yourself to a titch of embarrassment here and there; to practice resilience. Dance your goofiest in class. Make dumb jokes that only you laugh at…snorting… awkward… hard. Chat with a stranger in the coffee line. Perform a song for your students or the whole school. Do something you know you aren't perfect at in front of someone and take that first step out of the cage of perfectionism and into the fresh air of authenticity.

When we teachers show our students that our lovability and worthiness are not diminished by imperfections and mistakes, we finally create a space for the courage, adventure, and risk taking necessary to learn new things.

Your lovability and worthiness are not diminished by imperfections and mistakes! You are worthy of grace and understanding.

One of my favorite movies is *Serendipity* with John Cusack. He's taking a huge leap of faith and searching for signs to guide him in finding the woman of his dreams. He's about to give it up as a crazy venture when his best friend quotes Greek philosopher, Epictetus, "If you want to improve, be content to be thought foolish and stupid." He is inspired by Cusack's reckless pursuit of love even at the risk of being thought irresponsible. Our foolishness can encourage others wishing to take that leap, skip, or tiny hop of faith in pursuit of their own "silly dream." A happily flawed and imperfect teacher is the passageway for students to embrace their own flaws and imperfections (and those of their peers) as they join the journey to question everything and accept themselves and their foibles with love.

Room to screw up, drop some balls, and let shit go is key to really great teaching.

Happy screwing up, dear friend!

SKIPPING SCHOOL

R aise your hand if you're a teacher who feels like you're not doing enough; like you could be doing more.

PUT YOUR DARN HAND DOWN!

You've already done more than your fair share for the world. You are doing more than enough and the world is lucky to have you serving our learners of all ages. I'm here to tell you that you deserve support! American society, in particular, is so focused on independence, that we frame support as something we need rather than something we deserve.

I need therapy. I need a life coach. I need a doctor. I need physical therapy. The truth is I deserve therapy and healthcare the same way I deserve a massage or pedicure!

I left teaching to join the Peace Corps because of thoughtless and unreasonable rules and requests like being told to put a twenty page test booklet in front of my suicidal student with limited English skills, spending hours re-entering the same data four to five times because the district tech wasn't up to speed, being attacked for winning a grant without asking permission to apply for it first, and being forbidden to teach subtraction to students who still didn't understand the concept because it was not part of my assigned math curriculum. All of these insults on top of class size overload, idea overload, and work overload in general, led to the realization that my "job" was not humanly possible. But even more critical was the realization that, even if I did everything that was asked of me, some of it would actually be impairing learning. I decided early on that, in this line of work, I was going to have to challenge the status quo.

For five years, I whined a lot about my anxiety and stress but was absolutely not interested in investing time and money to transform my own well-being and joy which would have solved many of those problems. I used to think that time resting would only take me away from grading, planning, teacher evaluation portfolios, etc. — the very things that were giving me loads of chest-pain-level anxiety. I believed with absolute certainty that if I pushed harder and powered through with 60 to 80-hour work weeks and through the weekends, I would actually get it all done and feel great about what I had accomplished with students. Instead, I was sick all the time with monthly migraines, constant bladder infections, and whatever illnesses the students brought. I even signed myself up for anger management therapy when I finally realized that I didn't need to try to keep up and had already been giving more than my fair share; I deserved that kind of support.

I reached the depths of despair during a year that I had an unusual number of severely traumatized children: ambulance calls for suicide attempts, a student trying to dive off the desk onto the concrete floor because of hallucinations. One tried to slit another's throat with a nail file, and another had a psych evaluation suggesting he could become the next Ted Bundy. *This was a regular elementary classroom by the way.* I tried running miles every afternoon, attempting to let go of the worries I had for my students, worries that had nothing to do with academics. I knew something had to change.

I suddenly realized that I was socially conditioned to believe I had to use all of my time to make more money and produce more academic results. I had totally forgotten about my students other needs as well as my own! I was no longer spending time doing what I love; the things that called me to this profession. The book, *Drive*, by researcher and business guru, Daniel Pink, changed my life. This book taught me what 40 years of research suggests humans need to feel motivated. I had originally read it to bring more intrinsic motivation into my classroom, but I realized that I had the power to unlock my own intrinsic motivation too. All I needed to do was find small ways to claim autonomy over my time!

This was tricky in a career that has union rules, contracts, and is eyebrow deep in status quo. Who says I have to clock in at eight and leave at four? What if I can work it out to clock in at seven and leave at three? What if I want a two-hour lunch and am willing to stay late or come early for that? What if I don't want to clock in at all? Lots of companies, Patagonia for example, are ditching the traditional time clock in favor of a goal focused culture.

Laurie Santos, a professor at Yale University, who created the viral course called *The Science of Well-Being*, talks about time affluence. We hear the word affluence and automatically think of money. But in Santos' research, she has found that time affluence is key to happiness. Time affluence makes space for the other keys to being happy:

- Social connections
- Kindness
- Meditation
- Sleep
- Exercise

Do you pursue time the same way you pursue a paycheck? Did you know making more time will bring more happiness than making more money? I think I intuitively knew this but my mind is so much louder than my spirit.

One morning, after an incident with a student that I thought was going to land us on national news, I realized that I could not yoga my way out of this one and it was time to make a choice: to make time for rest, or quit mid-year. We had a three-day weekend coming up and I decided to give this time and rest stuff a try. I took my principal's offer for some mental health days and flew to Hawaii to lounge on the beach, visit with friends, eat, nap, swim, and lay on the beach some more. I didn't try to run around being a tourist. I was simply there to rest and absorb the beauty of that soul filling white beach and blue sky.

Just four days of rest worked so well that when I returned the next week, and tackled the pile I had left on my desk, it only took me two hours to accomplish what I thought would take two weeks. Pink and Santos were right, I realized that right away. It occurred to me then, that before my restful intervention I had been emotionally and mentally overwhelmed, and all of those wasted hours were making me slower and less efficient. I was working far beyond what I call my "efficiency level" and now saw the futility of powering through on caffeine and anger. If this worked so powerfully and quickly for me, what would the impact on my students be when I handed them over more autonomy (it was astounding; a total game changer but that's another conversation).

I knew that I needed to permanently grab hold of my time and put it to better use than working myself and my students into the ground. I had to set specific boundaries around time. You know those hours of planning time carved out where you have the best intention of getting your whole pile of grading done? You know how during that precious time, you can get sucked into chatting about the weekend, gossiping about colleagues, and sharing photos of other people's pets? (Or is that just me)? Yep, there goes all hope for actually getting anything done during my prep time.

I knew I needed to guard that time so I tried pulling the window blinds and locking my door so that it looked like no one was home but it still wasn't enough for me to get my stuff done efficiently and effectively. To reclaim autonomy over time when it seemed impossible, I renegotiated what my day would look like. It wasn't scary. I simply asked my administrator if I could try something different that was proven to increase motivation. I asked to work from home during extended planning days and rearranged my after-school hours to work better for my productivity and well-being. I knew that autonomy over time could make the most demoralized person feel empowered and valued again and I hoped it would do that for me. This token of trust from my principal went a long way to alleviate my sense of drowning in mandates and lifted me up in pursuit of a higher quality of life as a teacher.

For the rest of that year, I let go of the time spent on perceived **Have to's**, fears about test scores, and anything that wasn't time spent on contributing to building relationships with my students who had already experienced all types of trauma and abuse and who desperately needed an adult they could rely on. I hacked out time for rest and building relationships. It felt like a whole new world. I cared about my purpose. My students suddenly liked school. My soul for teaching was rejuvenated.

I claimed autonomy over my time by letting go of trying to "do it all" and instead, did the most important things better. No more 9PM nights planning and grading. No more weekends working on projects and data. I had spent years allowing my plate to be piled higher and higher, and I realized it was going to keep piling up as long as I kept saying "yes" and trying to do it all. My badass side lit up, and I noticed that I had some level of control over this. I realized my power to set boundaries and say, "No." My timers and alarms helped me get my butt out the door at quitting time. Alarms aren't just for getting out of bed. Have you noticed how much easier to respect the time boundary that says it's time to get up and get out the door TO school. But learning to honor that little bell when it means it's time to leave and take care of myself is much easier to ignore but dedication to my own health and happiness can't wait. Leaving work at school helped me honor my time away from work as sacred time for the other important parts of my life; the parts that ignite joy and passion. And, isn't an authentically passionate joyful teacher what students truly need? Joy and passion can't be faked. They must be nurtured. Let's start investing in that with serious integrity!

Convincing the principal wasn't the most challenging part of asking for more autonomy over my time. It was when colleagues saw me teaching the last twenty minutes in my snow pants and running out the door with the kids to throw my board on my car and head to the mountains. Some thought I was slacking; others were inspired.

I hadn't been carving out after school time very long when our school hired a new counselor. One afternoon she saw me fly out the door with my students in full snow gear. She went into our staff lounge and said to the group at the table, "Do you know what Jamie just did? She ran outside, threw her snowboard on top of her car and took off!" The teachers there responded, "Yeah, she does that." Our counselor said in amazement, "That's so healthy!"

The difference between the new counselor and those that couldn't grasp the concept of how time for play was benefiting my students was a mindset that values the pursuit of well-being as an important part of doing good work and good teaching. The criticism was hurtful but I was reaping the rewards of making time for play and self-care and it was quickly improving student learning and my life. I learned that just because something is fun and enjoyable doesn't diminish its importance to those we serve. I had a duty to be out there enjoying the mountain, cutting the chords of stress and frustration so that I could return the next day with patience, kindness, empathy, and mental clarity. These characteristics are the currency of learning.

It wasn't until I started building my time affluence and using it to live like I mattered more than test scores, evaluations, and the pile on my desk that I was able to help my students feel like they were worth more than mandates and minutia. When teachers are taken care of, it ripples out to our students in a powerful way.

I know that when I set rock solid boundaries around time for rest and personal well-being practices, I became so much more resourceful and efficient that my to do list (which I don't do anymore) took less than half the time it had taken before. I can't emphasize enough that;

There is no training or curriculum that will impact students the way happy teachers will.

After all, if we accept an educational culture that normalizes the demoralization, overwhelm and exhaustion of it's educators, what, really, are we offering students? This is why time for my well-being practices and personally meaningful work are two of the non-negotiable items I keep on my list. The baby steps I took began with setting a timer at 8PM and no matter what still wasn't finished, I put it away, poured a glass of wine and got out a good book or movie. Over a few years, I slowly backed that "wine-down" time up to dinner time and eventually an hour after school was out so that I had much more time to love my life.

Another baby step, was taking my breaks. I would walk to a local coffee shop during recess and treat myself at least once a week to my favorite latte. One final baby step was leaving my bag of unfinished work in the car instead of bringing it into the house until I eventually felt comfortable leaving it at school.

Once I wholeheartedly embraced leaving at a reasonable time, taking mental health days, and resting without guilt or worry about what still needed to be done in the bog of eternal paperwork, I became a happier, healthier, more successful teacher, friend, lover, sister, daughter, woman.

GETTING NAKED

"She's NAKED!!!" I screamed into the midnight pine scented forest. My voice echoed through the mountains as she gracefully and without inhibition stepped into the steaming and overflowing hot tub full of naked teachers.

Each winter we would have a retreat at a friend's rustic little cabin snuggled into the woods. Sometimes there would be ten of us crammed together, sleeping on couches and floors for the chance to enjoy this time to play games, decompress, share our most embarrassing moments and create a few new ones together. There is a kind of trust only being naked together can create. A trust that there is no judgement. A trust that holds your vulnerability with respect and honor. A trust that is fun and playful.

Jump forward to the next school year and the hot tub crew is being introduced to our new school counselor. While introducing herself to us and explaining the importance of teamwork and coming together during adversity, our new counselor used the analogy of "getting naked" together and we all fought back the flood of giggles bubbling up in our tummies. The counselor noticed the collective gasp. We all started giving each other sideways glances and there was a collective pressure building as we held in our laughter. The counselor asked, "Am I missing something?" Someone blurted out, "We HAVE gotten naked together!" And the laughter flowed uncontrollably, gloriously through the room. This counselor was quickly absorbed into our tribe.

For a group of women to let go of our body image fears is the truest expression of our total freedom from judgement and our faith in each other. It's a place we know we are absolutely welcome to come as we are with all our imperfections and secrets laid bare. You matter more than fears and insecurities; your own or those of your most harsh critics.

So...who gets you? Who can you "get naked" with at your school? Ok, ok. Maybe not literally. It's not for everyone, though I absolutely do recommend it. My point is; for us to thrive, we gotta build our tribe. We talk about "finding" a tribe but that's not always how it goes. Sometimes it means taking the reins in my own hands and building up a tribe within a new community.

Why do I need a team? Why can't I just shut my door and do my thing? If "shut the door and teach" is your thing, check in with yourself and ask:

Is this making me supremely happy at work?
Am I getting what I need to be able show up for my students and teach with my highest integrity?

If the answers are yes, cool, do your thing and be ready for someone who really wants your confident self in their tribe. If no, you're not alone.
Doris Santoro, in her book *Demoralized*, proves that professional community is the core of teacher longevity. Everything else springs from the relationships in this professional community.

As the anonymous philosopher says, "If you want to go fast, go alone. If you want to go far, go together."

You are worthy of a supportive community!

What are some small steps to identify your allies and build up those alliances? Start with taking time to think about all of the people who make up your community: parents, students, teachers, administration, staff, organizations, classes, civic groups, policymakers, etc. Who's got your back? If no one yet, who can you get to know better? If you are at a school where no one eats lunch in the staff lounge (a sure sign of an unhealthy culture), eat in a common area by yourself until one other person joins you, then another, then another.

You can team up for anything and it's best to start small and low vulnerability/professional risk: book clubs, coffee, sit together at meetings, start a Friday soup club, share teaching materials, attend interesting classes or conferences together, chat during bus duty, make small connections. Starting with something with high professional risk, such as, getting a big decision overturned for your whole district before you have tested the waters of friendship and built at least a tentative trust, can result in arguments and frustration that damage the professional community.

My shoulders sagged the lowest with loneliness and discouragement when starting in a new school that had built a culture based on extreme competition and shame. At first, I struggled to get people to even to acknowledge my, "Good morning." Few people talked to each other. Finding my allies took a lot of small tokens of trust as simple as smiles, eye contact, and a cup of coffee here and there to show my support before I could build a team that worked together.

Consider who might team up with you for a mission that is small and fun. There are so many fun music videos teachers have teamed up on to welcome students back to virtual school during this year of COVID. I'm sure there was lots of laughter; the kind of laughter that glues you together for many more missions to come.

I once hosted a "Tatas for Teachers" bra decorating party in my classroom for a community breast cancer awareness event. The people who showed up and brought art supplies, extra bras, and snacks were instantly on my team. You could also try something like starting "Beverage committee meetings" on Friday at your favorite happy hour spot. I've been part of a social committee that kept track of birthdays and important events to celebrate our staff. Teachers deserve to be celebrated! Once I've tested out these simple waters of team work and things have gone well, I'm ready to move to the next level.

A mid-level joint effort in my elementary school was to team up and tackle all of the literary elements to be covered. Each teacher took one element and we traded students for an hour each day until all students had learned all of the elements. That way we each develop and hone one precisely crafted lesson over and over until we become the hands down expert on that topic. You could do the same for any subject that feels cumbersome. Tribes SHARE the load! Once we trusted each other enough to go wine tasting, and paint bras together, trusting each other with workloads and students is a natural and deeply satisfying progression. A solid team feeds our need for meaningful connection and creates more time to make a run for the washroom.

Another benefit of a solid team is a more powerful voice at the decision-making table. The highest level functioning teams, strongly united, can take bigger professional risks to improve the integrity of their school with more confidence and more success. In my experience, a team reaches this level after three years of working together well.

Year one, you get to know each other's quirks and philosophies. You learn to laugh together and dip your toe in the water. Year two, you share each other's work loads and build trust. You're probably ready to hot tub in your underwear. Year three, you're ready to go full noodle naked. You take on policy changes and even protest with confidence knowing that you absolutely stand together. Teachers are not handed a seat at the decision-making table so it takes a little more effort to carve a path to that sacred space.

With my teams, I have challenged mandated policy around time, testing, and curriculum. Refusing to assign a team leader to our grade-level team was one of the most energy consuming. Our district required one person at each grade level to regularly attend district meetings about testing and data. We noticed quickly these district wide meetings were focused on fear of test scores and set in place harmful mandates like testing in English only. I had to stick to my pledge to teach with integrity even when I was sweating bullets in the hot seat of intimidation and threats. We researched our rights and knew that we could lawfully refuse this mandate in our effort to hold up the integrity of our profession and give precedence to the wellbeing of our students.

We stood together as a team and refused to participate in the district wide fear mongering any longer. We, instead, embraced long-standing research and evidence to take the ethical high ground, digging deep into what we knew our students needed and creating a plan of action for learning to move forward, now free to shift our focus away from lack and deficit and instead focus on growth and success.

Our teamwork led to other schools around the state taking notice and contacting or visiting us for advice on how to improve their own collaboration.

This level of collaboration cannot be fear driven. It only happens when courageous people are willing to come together under adversity and stand firm for the integrity of our profession and benefit of our students.

Remember, your tribe does not have to be a grade level team. You can step outside your grade level or subject area and with this diverse representation have an even more powerful voice. Santoro is very clear in her book, *Demoralized*, that for teachers to be willing to engage in professional risk, we must be in a professional community of our choosing. That means professional learning communities that are pre-assigned by grade level or subject area may not be as effective as choosing your own people with common interests and goals, such as literacy, leadership, community, diversity and equity, or policy change. The best person to decide what you want to study and add to your skill set is YOU, not an administrator or principal. You deserve to pursue your passions. You do not need fear or competition snapping a whip behind you. There may be more risk negotiating new teams — teams based on passion and goals but research confirms it will increase your motivation for teaching immensely!

In the end, I'm sitting here writing this book two years after leaving the traditional classroom to start my own business. The scariest part of writing a book is that someone will actually read it! This is a new level of naked for me. Who are my allies and who is my tribe in this situation? I have learned that my biggest risks in life have always included allies; family, friends, colleagues, students, and people that seem to pop up out of nowhere, waving a flag of solidarity and support for my mission.

When I made the decision to leave my stable teaching career to join the Peace Corps, I learned that for me to go out on a limb, I needed a strong and deeply rooted tree to support that feeble and precarious limb. Those that stayed home and sent care packages, words of encouragement, and shared my story acted as my rooted tree. They supported the wobbly vulnerable limb I was inching out onto as I left a salary, health benefits, and home.

My tree-tribe for writing this book includes, a favorite college English instructor, Jack Johnson, helping me remember to write out the darn small numbers, one…two…three, my dad making sure my voice shines through, my family filling me with encouragement and knowledge that even if this goes badly, they will still love me, forty-six brilliant teachers from a couple different Facebook grous that I've never met who are reviewing chapters as I write this, and a team of friends helping me market this book. I even reached out on Facebook to decide on the cover and received ten thousand responses! I started asking for people to be on my team in all directions to see who wanted to join the fun. And now, I've got my tribe; my partners in crime. They are all waving the flag of my mission to remind the world that teachers matter more than test scores and unfair standards. I have proven to myself that the research stands true. In every situation, my tribe is key to being empowered and staying healthy.

My question for you is, who waves a flag for you? Do

people know what your mission is or what you stand for? Do you? You deserve a whole parade of flags and fan-fare shouting your anthem and holding you up. Whether your cause is more time to pee or better coffee for the staff lounge, you deserve support and there ARE people out there who are eager to join your movement.

The moral of this story is *find your allies* even if that means looking at a different school or in a new town or not in school at all. Find them through chats, book clubs, coffee, and small connections. Simply say, *hi*. Find a flag you can wave together. You are a gift and you deserve to be with the people who appreciate you as that perfect gift. You deserve people who are a gift to you. Gather and surround yourself with helpful people, courageous people, the people you could joyfully share a hot tub with...naked.

A TEACHER WITH A VOICE...

If they don't give you a seat at the table, bring a folding chair.

—SHIRLEY CHISHOLM

My mission is a world of happy teachers. To accomplish this, I know fist hand the importance of addressing bullying at work. Sometimes the problem is bigger than being excluded; it's being disregarded and silenced at the decision making table. Morten Birkeland Nielsen & Ståle Einarsen, long time researchers on bullying in the workplace, explain the way bullying plays a role in:

> *mental and physical health problems, symptoms of post-traumatic stress, burnout, increased intentions to leave, and reduced job satisfaction and organizational commitment. ... absenteeism, performance, self-perceptions, and sleep.*

Bullying isn't confined to the playground. It is aggressive behavior that recurs persistently over time where there is a real or perceived power imbalance, and can come from superiors or co-workers alike. Bullies gain control over their targets by keeping them quiet.

As a teacher, I experienced every single one of the named effects of bullying. I was calling in sick a lot because being around my bullies was like keeping my balance on my paddle board as a shark slowly circled beneath me and this stress would physically manifest itself as migraines and vomiting. I became so angry all the time that friends started to notice, and express concern. I signed myself up for therapy in hopes of lifting myself out of "the trenches."

Being heard and speaking out, whether in a loud confident voice or a timid shaky voice is the direct opposite of being bullied by those in favor of status quo and apathy. In fact, in her book *Demoralized*, Doris A. Santoro, professor of education and researcher at Bowdoin College, names voice as a determining factor for teacher retention. This old story popped into my mind when in her foreword, Santoro explains how, "...Voices raised by experienced and admired classroom teachers... are neither heard nor respected."

I was only a couple of years into my teaching career in Washington State. I was at a union letter writing event and one of the speakers announced to us all that when writing a letter to the governor (whom she used to work for) we should never sign our own name or mention that we are a teacher. She said that she was personally instructed during her time in the governor's office to ignore letters about education from teachers and send only canned responses! She suggested having family or community members send our letters. Fifteen years later, I wrote a letter to our governor and received the exact same canned letter my father received in the 80's! The budget issue I was asking about in my letter, apparently hadn't changed one penny in all that time.

On the other hand, I have also received an email to all National Board Certified Teachers to please stop emailing the state senate as they passed a bill addressing the issue we were kicking and screaming about with unified voices and to start sending those emails to the house. It felt great to be a part of so many strong active voices loud enough to be heard and effect change. I don't even remember what we were trying to get passed but that email showed me how loud we can be together.

Regardless of whether or not teacher voices are heard or respected, the BELIEF that one is not or will never be heard is demoralizing. This disempowering thought and belief sucks away the motivation to speak up at all.

What can a teacher do at the school or district level to be heard? If I want to claim time to pee, I'm may have to kick and scream for it a bit!

❖ ❖ ❖

When I first went into teaching, I truly believed I would have the chance to empower kids to question everything and LOVE learning. I still remember the day I was handed my first script to teach reading. I was subbing in an elementary classroom, and it was literally a *Teacher says/ Students say:...* scripted curriculum. I already had my Master's degree in literacy and knew from research that this practice was not good for students and was downright insulting to me. I thought, "WTF?!! Just because I'm a sub they think I need a script to do my job?"

You can imagine how crushed I was to discover that this script was not only required for substitutes, but all teachers, district wide, were expected to teach using those robotic methods; devoid of any freedom, autonomy, or trust in our professional capabilities and in direct contradiction to what research says is best for learning.

Scripts were just the beginning of my descent into demoralization. I felt blessed to be a teacher but I was not having the impact I knew I had the potential to create.

So often in teaching, it can feel like we have no voice, our voice doesn't matter, and we will never be considered at the decision-making table. The world of education is notoriously full of bullies who silence our ethical concerns. It often feels like the teacher is no longer respected as a well-educated professional with years of specialized training, and viewed more as a workhorse. New evidence, still to be published this coming September from Lisa Surkovich, a doctoral student at Indiana University of Pennsylvania, shows that "administrative factors" are the main source of teacher stress and that to stay in the profession and beat the burnout teachers must have respect, support and more autonomy. More and more research is showing that leaders and policy makers in education have a direct make or break impact on a teacher's ability to remain in the profession.

Since this book is written directly to the teacher, rather than leaders, policy makers or administrators, this is a call to teachers to share the current research on burnout, demoralization, and teacher flight with leaders, colleagues, on your blogs, and in letters to your lawmakers! Not many people are looking these things up right now. I researched the keywords to see who is actually searching for information on teacher burnout and flight on platforms like Google. The numbers were insanely low which means that the strategies being employed to support overwhelmed teachers may not be researched based... hot dog trucks for the day, decorations in the staff room and goofy dances at staff meetings don't cut it. We need to make sure leaders know what DOES WORK!

So, let's talk about those policy makers and their policies... Policies are sneaky. I know I forget they are changeable sometimes. The word "policy" has come to mean "the way it is — end of story."

But, "That's the way it's always been done." has never been a good enough reason for me to keep doing it that way, whatever "it" may be. Looking back through my career. I'm thrilled to find a long record of policy changes that I was honored to be a part of — policies that created much more equity and ease. This happens through building a courageous voice one terrified and trembling word at a time. It means moving passed bullies up toward their bosses and continuing upward with that voice. It means being willing to be fired to maintain your integrity. Dr. Adeyemi Stembridge told me in a book study I was facilitating on his book, Culturally Responsive Education in the Classroom, that "if you aren't fired at least once, you aren't really trying."

At the time, it usually felt like I was kicking and screaming for policy change and getting nowhere with policy makers, but after some time intentionally reflecting on my career, every single policy that was deeply important to me, was changed. Sometimes it took a month and sometimes it took five years. Many of those policies have now spread into the larger system outside of my school and even into other districts.

Most of my kicking and screaming was to gain equity for my students, but I also kicked and screamed for staff equity and the integrity of the teaching profession. It was exhausting at times and was like bushwhacking through a jungle of bullies, abuse, and apathy but I knew that this path to paradise was worth the effort. It would bring my fellow teachers, people I admired and loved, out of a culture of fear and failure and into a powerful sense of worthiness with the freedom to take bathroom breaks whenever we wanted. I knew it was the time to put MY oxygen mask on first, and once I was breathing easy, I could then help others catch their breath. But, which specific policies was I involved in changing? That's coming...

First, I want to share the main point of this chapter;

*Don't believe the lie that
you have no voice.*

Find the right people to kick and scream to or with. Don't believe it's hopeless.

When I'm feeling powerless, I make room for myself to throw a little tantrum and then try not to hang out in that mindset too long. I don't want to get stuck there. So, after letting off some steam, I seek some sort of inspiration like a Super Soul Sunday with Oprah. Then, I ask myself, how CAN I be heard? Who WILL listen? I let go of my fears around how much it will piss off the bullies in my life who are trying to censor and diminish my voice. I don't have time for bullies, my patience is wasted on them. My students need me and I need policies that lead to enjoying my life and work. I deserve that and so do you!

I learned that "the keys to my happiness are in my own pocket" and to value myself as a professional who has a right to the space to speak up and be heard. Being heard is vital to a teacher's sense of purpose and value. To develop a sense of purpose and value, I pursue my chance to be heard.

I bushwhacked my way to being heard when I wanted testing in Spanish for my bilingual students. I had students from Mexico, new to the U.S., who were being given math tests in English! I was outraged because they were legally entitled to test in their native language and we had access to the same normed math test in Spanish. It was a simple matter of clicking the Spanish test option on the computer and off they would go.

I was directed to give the test in English despite my expressed concerns. *There was no choice,* I was told. *The data would be too hard to sort out.* I was given any number of excuses. But I knew it would save me and my students time throughout the school year if I could use the test to determine what they actually needed to learn in math rather than repeating concepts they already knew but couldn't yet demonstrate in a new language. So, the first time I gave the darn test in English and re-administered the test in Spanish the next day. For one student this resulted in a three-year improvement in his scores. He was actually a year above grade level in math! Even with this evidence in hand, I was still told I could not use the Spanish test.

At this point, I decided that I would not give into this form of oppression only to preserve the comfortable status quo. I gave the Spanish test anyway…

year after year until it became policy in my district. I was questioned and chastised every time. My principal did her best to support my mission because she knew it was right. My voice was not heard but my actions were. When I refused to subject my students and myself to such inequity for the sake of status quo and easier data keeping, I was given permission to be the ONLY teacher in the district who could give the correct test but they would not count my scores in district wide data. Testing in Spanish was eventually implemented district wide over the course of a couple of years. Accurate assessments were a big part of how I carved out time to pee. Pointless tests waste everyone's time and can be emotionally damaging to those being forced to take them.

My voice, though often shaking and trembling, stood by me when...

> I wanted teacher teams to decide where students are placed, both at the beginning of the year and for new enrollments, instead of our office secretary (who already had more than enough piled on her desk).
>
> When I refused to add "school interpreter" to my already full plate as a teacher.
>
> When I wanted to desegregate my bilingual classroom. This meant carefully planning and using data to map out classroom demo-

graphics rather than throwing any student with a LAS score in my room.

When I wanted intervention classes to be smaller than enrichment classes.

When I refused to plan lessons for other certified teachers.

When I stood my ground to not take more than eight students while developing a new alternative program.

When I stood up against spending an extra twenty hours per week entering data for our district.

When I refused to check email and messages over the weekend and after hours.

Every time I set my non-negotiable values and practices at the freaking interview table and stuck to them!

I'm the one in charge of respecting my boundaries and that means standing firm in the face of some vicious attacks. It's better to live through five minutes of hell having a difficult conversation than to trudge through decades of misery because of fear and the resignation that I can "just live with it." If it's not going well, don't worry, that's because you're doing it right. They feel your new boundary and are pushing back until they realize, you're not budging.

Michelle Summers, a teacher and motivational speaker from Montgomery Alabama, shared (in a Facebook live post that went viral) a controversial decision made by her school district during the 2020 COVID pandemic.

June 26th, 2020: "We can't go into work because an incident...with one of our coworkers testing positive (and we've all been around them). But because we were required to come [to school] because as it was stated to us they didn't want us to get out of the habit of going to work. So we needed to come back to work and now we have people testing positive on our campus... it could spread like wildfire."

Michelle makes a powerful argument for including experienced teachers at the decision-making table. This is a policy that needs to be changed globally. I'm certain that with active and experienced teachers joining the decision-making table and designing education policies, resource gaps will close, teacher flight will end, and equity will finally be a part of education. Without the teachers driving the decisions, we continue to suffer under best guesses, unrecognized bias, and harmful status quo. In the smaller system of a school, the change can start with a simple shift in mindset.

This mindset among school leaders that "we don't want staff to get used to not coming in to work" says that "we, the leaders of this organization, believe you, who work for us, are inherently lazy and if we don't keep your feet to the fire, you don't have what it takes to be passionate and dedicated to this profession."

When any leader (whether teacher, parent, or president) stands on the foundation that their people are lacking or lazy, it harms the culture and the productivity of that society. Similar to what happens to people who are bullied at work, as mentioned in the quote at the beginning of this chapter, abuse leads to calling in sick and losing interest in work. This deficit mindset is what creates hopelessness disguised as laziness. People who are told they are inept start to believe they are inept, and then behave that way. People who are traumatized are more likely to exhibit problematic behavior than people who are not.

When a leader stands on a foundation that recognizes the potential, possibility, and assets (which I like to call superpowers) in the people they are leading, those leaders get remarkable results and have a lasting impact on the culture of their organization. People who are uplifted and celebrated begin to uplift and celebrate others. They become dedicated to their work and see it as more than a job.

So how does a teacher manifest this shift in school culture? Practice it in your classroom, with parents, and colleagues. It happens one person at a time.

I have had this very conversation about shifting to an asset based mindset with several leaders and a few of my own superiors. Every time, I've seen an immediate, sometimes overnight, turnaround in the culture of the organization they lead. I invite you to use your voice to shift the mindsets and policies that lead to silencing teacher voices. Teacher's deserve policies that empower them at the decision-making table and so do students.

❖ ❖ ❖

Being heard is a ton of emotional labor. Learning to choose your battles and pace yourself is key. If possible, don't do it alone. Start small. In the end, it's worse to spend an entire career suffering under harmful policies than it is to spend a few weeks sending emails and sweating in some difficult meetings. Build your courage and your voice one ethical battle at a time. Don't try to do it all at once; small steps over time mean you can maintain your joy and stamina.

So, what are some of those small steps? There are three strategies that have worked for me.

Strategy 1

First, and most importantly, **speak up**! Broadcast your concerns and repeat them as many times as it takes to be heard. I talk to colleagues, I raise my hand (a lot) at meetings, I talk to families, I get on the phone, and then I schedule more meetings.

> *"When we speak we are afraid our words*
> *will not be heard or welcomed. But when*
> *we are silent, we are still afraid.*
> *So it is better to speak."*
> *- Audre Lorde, Activist, Teacher, Adventurer*

Walk around with your message and your mission on a sticky note stuck to your forehead. I keep it to ONE mission at a time. I won't change anything if I burn out trying to save the whole world at once. Trust the slow and intentional process.

Strategy 2

The second trick to being heard is **email** and other digital forms of communication. This modality can be tricky and easily misunderstood. I use email as a megaphone in several different ways. I use it to document conversations and agreements that can be lost amongst the maddening schedules of many school leaders and policy makers. When I write an email about a hot topic of concern, I have a rule to keep it to four sentences max. If I need more than that, I use those four sentences to initiate a face-to-face meeting or phone call.

I also almost never (again, I'm not perfect) send an email when I'm still breathing flames or have my eyes popping out of my head. I pay attention. If my mouth is hanging open, I don't send it. When I absolutely need to vent, I draft an email but I don't send anything until, at least, the next day. (While drafting I leave the "To:" field blank so I don't accidentally send my draft before I'm ready).

One more thing to remember: when the topic feels like a professional risk, I include or cc at least two people in the email. I avoid one on one conversations about hot topics to ensure the safety and accountability of myself and my colleagues or superiors. Having a third party does two things; it keeps the communication cordial, and it holds everyone accountable for their decisions, information, and tone.

Remember, stick to one mission at a time. I remind myself that my goal is to create MORE time to pee and I know that a cause can suck away that time if I'm not intentional with my approach and emotional labor.

Strategy 3

The last and most daring step I take in resisting the toxic status quo is mustering the courage to **climb high**. Too many teachers are shackled to the chain of command. I refuse to live in fear of bad leadership. Fear-based leadership, AKA bullying/abuse, has no place in education or in any workplace for that matter.

If I'm struggling with unfair mandates or hitting irrational roadblocks like continued denial of requests without valid reasons (yes, as a professional, you do deserve a conversation about any reasons your reasonable requests are denied, "Because I said so" doesn't cut it), I do my research making sure that getting a rule or decision changed is the right thing to do. Like a lawyer my foundational argument must withstand any attacks. Then, I find a way around, over, under, or through the roadblock. I don't take the first or even the 27th "no" if I know something is deeply unjust and holding back student learning, my health, or my happiness as a professional. Sometimes that has meant letting go of a toxic workplace and looking for work at another organization or even founding my own business.

Speaking out to a higher authority is especially important if you are in a toxic environment. In his blog, *Psychology of self*, Darius Cikanavicius, a psychological consultant and a certified mental health coach, names key reasons we stay silent about abuse in the workplace. They are:

- Normalization
- Minimization
- Shame

- Fear
- Isolation
- Betrayal
- Lack of support

In our society, so much of what should be openly considered abuse is normalized. Narcissistic behavior is normalized as "competition" or "high self-esteem," physical abuse of children as "discipline," neglect as "character building," intimidation as "being assertive," triangulation as "seeking support," character assassination as "telling the truth," bullying as "just joking," gaslighting as "just my side of the story" or "alternative facts/truth," and so on.

So, when people say that they've been abused, their experiences are not recognized as traumatic. Many instances of abuse are simply brushed off as "normal," which makes the person feel even more invalidated and traumatized.

◆ ◆ ◆

Most leaders and policy makers I have worked with

fight the same battles I have and share in the exhaustion that had my mind on a never ending hamster wheel causing me to sing Yellow Submarine on repeat (I know it's time to meditate when I start frantically humming that song. Not sure where it came from). It is essential that I empower myself by empowering my colleagues and supervisors; I spoil them the way I would love to be spoiled as a valued professional, loved for my superpowers (assets).

One of my pet peeves is hearing the words, "We value you" and then being served cold rubber hot dogs from the cafeteria for our big district event. Food in many cultures, including the US, says a lot about how we feel about our guests. Are we offering something that takes no time, or thought? Does it have any nutritional value? At a very large Marzano conference in Seattle, many of the participants complained that the entire breakfast we were promised, had 0 protein options. It was all muffins and donuts with no real fuel to start the day. We felt neglected because this menu showed very little concern for the health and enjoyment of the guests who would need fuel to sustain our brains for long days of hardcore learning.

So, in contrast, I find ways to demonstrate the value that I hold for my colleagues, supervisors, and students. While a fully catered event isn't in my budget as a teacher, for the one-on-one or small meeting, here's what I do…

Here, in the Pacific Northwest, coffee cards are like cigarettes in prison and when the need arises I never hesitate to make it rain coffee. When someone fills out a cumbersome form, spends time helping me cut a hole in my cupboard to hide the chord of the microwave that isn't allowed in my classroom, or comes to one more of the stinking meetings I insisted on, I make darn sure they know I appreciate them and their support. Whether they are my superior or not, they get some love from me in the form of gourmet coffee out or in a card form, chocolate, or even sometimes…lunch. This show of appreciation gives our relationship a boost. It is empowering to model and set a precedent that honors our effort and profession as educators.

I realized that I'm not in this work just for the money or the benefits. It's worth risking losing my job to love my job. I know that teachers are in short supply now because so many are fleeing the abuse and shaming that feels like it comes at us from every direction. And, I know that we deserve to find a place that values what we have to offer, and will welcome our voices at the table. I reject the lies that a place like that doesn't exist and that no one wants to hear us. I've begun to live in the truth that teacher voices are worthy of being heard. Your voice is vital to the integrity of this profession.

FEEL NO GUILT

Feel no guilt. Getting married and giving birth [or teaching] does not mean that you have sold your life away to perfectly healthy people who can get their own damn socks [or pencils].

— JENNIFER CRUSIE

I attended leadership camp during my senior year of high school, where I won "The best frying bacon" acting contest. It was a moment where I deeply embraced letting go of what other people think and I really channeled the bacon as it transforms from a cold, thin piece of greasy meat to a popping, spitting, twitching strip of hot deliciousness in a black cast-iron pan. That trip was the beginning of my transformational life coaching path. The breakthrough I had at camp that summer was that a good leader doesn't "do for" others. A good leader shows others the way to do for themselves. That has been the foundation of my teaching and life coaching my entire adult life. It helped me let go of the guilt and fear of judgement that comes from daring to be myself (frying like bacon) or from refusing to carry people over the finish line. I learned that when I chase the hero card all the time, I never leave room for others to be their own hero.

As I looked more closely at what I was calling guilt, I noticed it came with excuses and little white lies. Thoughts like, *This would all fall apart if I weren't handling it,* show how little confidence we have in the people around us. Either I have not done the work of teaching others to handle their roles well, or I'm automatically assuming no one cares, or has the capacity to care, about "what needs to be done." And, if no one else really does care, then why do I, and why the heck am I forcing people to care about something they are not interested in? Why am I pushing for something to exist, or function, or happen when I am the **only** one who cares if it exists, or functions, or happens? Yes, sometimes this is being the innovator and sometimes it's something to let go.

A teacher client was obsessing over making Prom happen in the year of COVID. Understandably, no one else seemed interested so she kept taking on more and more responsibility until she realized, *no one cares about prom and I'm making myself miserable doing all this work I've guilted myself into.* She decided to just take a break, relieve herself of the poison that misplaced guilt always brings, and the world didn't come to an end. She finally allowed herself to let go, and no one hated her. I don't know if prom happened or not, but I do saw the relief that came to her face when she realized she could breathe again. Guilt can act as a red warning flag to signal when it's time to differentiate between what is expected and what is important.

When I'm on a mission to bring joy and autonomy into a life, I'm not willing to drag people down the street toward what I deem is best for them. Do you know what people being dragged down the street do when you let go? They lay there. Who am I to decide that laying there is not exactly what they need right now? Sometimes that IS exactly what they need. Guilt tells me *I can't let them fail* but that is my pride talking. *How will I look if they fail? I know better than they do. They just don't get it.* These thoughts only disempower the people I love and care about.

Letting go of guilt means having faith in people and their own divine path. It means allowing life to be as it is and being there to support and facilitate growth, learning, and joy as people become ready for those things while not taking personal ownership of those things for others.

Letting go of guilt looks like giving gleefully. If I say *yes* when I mean *no* or give something away that I really wanted to keep, I'm not being truly generous because I'm stealing something from myself. I won't feel happy about what I'm offering. Instead I harbor resentment and anger. If I say yes, when I mean yes with a glad heart and I give when it's so exciting that it makes me fill with light and butterflies, then I am truly guilt free and giving from a place of love. And no trying to fake myself out with what I think I "should" want. Authenticity is vital. Practicing the courage to say no is as charitable and generous as saying yes because that's what showing up as the best me looks like. If I judge myself as selfish, weak, or lazy for not giving and doing things I don't want to do, that guilt and self-judgement will only create more obstacles to becoming my best self. No one says this better than the activist, philanthropist, and author Glennon Doyle during her interview on the podcast, *Unlocking Us*, with Brené Brown:

> *I think that one of the poison roots that were planted beneath women [and teachers] is the idea that if we do what is best for us, that if we do what we need to do, what we want to do, our people will be hurt. We have accepted this lie that what we need and what our people need is mutually exclusive. And that is a lie.*

What is true and beautiful for us is always ultimately what is true and beautiful for our people because there's no such thing as one way liberation. When we free ourselves, we automatically free everyone around us. When we grant ourselves permission to live as our truest selves, we automatically grant permission to everyone around us to do the same because freedom is contagious.

The truth of this came to me when caring for my mother during her open-heart surgery. I discovered the importance of brushing my teeth. It's a simple self-care habit that most people don't struggle to take time for. Normally, I'm super regular about brushing and flossing and for some reason taking time to find a place in the hospital to do this simple bit of self-care felt impossible. How could I leave my mom after she just had her chest cracked open, her heart, stopped and cut into, so that I can brush my freaking teeth? Who cares about my teeth? Well, here's the thing I realized.

I can give up brushing my teeth in favor of caring for my loved ones. But then, my breath will be bad and they won't want kisses or conversations with me anymore. If I don't brush my teeth, eventually I will start to have pain from cavities. That pain will make me impatient and angry and I will start to hurt the feelings of those I'm trying to love and care for.

My pain will push them away. When my teeth start to rot, I will get sick and the people I was supposed to be sacrificing for and taking such great care of will now be taking care of a very sick and miserable me. If a simple self-care task like brushing my teeth can lead to such a disaster, what can something like doctors visits, emotional support, and committing to soul-filling time in the mountains do to make me the best warrior of love I can be?!!

When I did finally make time to brush my teeth and even take a nap, it was like a day at the spa; total luxury. I was able to come back to my mother's hospital room emitting joy and positive energy. I also relieved my dad to take a break and revive his own body and spirit and so the ripple of care spreads. Your rest and care matter more than your fear of judgment and guilt!

Letting go of guilt means letting go of pride and embracing a humble spirit. When I rest in humility, there is no guilt. I remember that the world is not spinning because of me and it will not collapse without my efforts to rescue everyone. Making more room for people to be their own hero leaves space for them to discover their own miracles and growth.

Letting go of guilt means believing in others. It means assessing what is important to others from their actions and conversations rather than my own assumptions, and worse yet, according to what I decide is best.

Letting go of the guilt associated with trying to do everything for everyone, looks like patience while people learn to do things on their own. It looks like faith that people can rise up again even when they fail because failure is part of success. It looks like accepting approximation and not having it all go my way. It looks like letting go of a scarcity mindset that believes I'm dropping balls and letting people down when I allow them to pick themselves up and carry their own weight.

Letting a few balls drop does not make me less reliable. Refusing to keep all of those balls flying in the air makes me more reliable because I'm not spreading myself so thin that everything I do is half-assed. Instead, I make time to do a few important things consistently and with excellence. The only reason the balls drop in the first place is not a reflection on my juggling skills. It's because someone tried to throw extra balls at me without making sure I was ready or first asking for my permission (we learn that in Kindergarten P.E.). The person throwing those balls at me without making sure I want them, and am willing to juggle them, is the one who is truly dropping the ball.

My automatic reflex to a ball being thrown at me is to try and catch it. So, I have to teach myself to stay focused on what I'm already juggling and allow that flying missile of "more to do" bounce right off me and roll away. Knowing when to say "No" is the foundation of reliability even over showing up!

Letting go of guilt means I love the people in my life, and who I serve, enough to pursue rest and self-care practices that will ensure I can show up at my best more often.

Why is doing the work of letting go of guilt important to teaching and still having time to pee? Brené Brown, the great story teller and shame researcher, says in her podcast, *Unlocking Us*, "When we are insecure and unhappy we are afraid to be wrong, vulnerable, or authentic." —All the things people we care for need from us. All the things we need for ourselves. A happy me is the most loving me. I won't have the energy or spirit to take a stand for my well-being and healthy boundaries if I let pride, perfectionism, and fear that show up as guilt hold me back. If I hold onto guilt there will be less room for joy and love in my heart and I won't glow with my most brilliant light. Guilt blinds you to your highest purpose and blocks the way to success because you don't allow yourself to deserve it; guilt withholds grace!

Have you heard of the crabs in the basket story? There's a basket of crabs that have been captured waiting to become a delicious gourmet meal. As one crab starts to crawl out of the basket and is almost over the lip and about to reach the beach to run toward an ocean of freedom, the other crabs grab her legs and pull her back down. The captors don't even bother to put a lid on a basket of crabs because their own "society" keeps them trapped in the basket. Guilt is the mass of crabs in the basket pulling my free-spirited self back into captivity even as I see clearly and attempt to pursue a path to freedom.

So, when I feel my heart tighten and my breath shorten as I suffocate with guilt from saying "no," or for taking a walk in the forest instead of grading papers —when I think I'm not worthy of rest because I haven't worked hard enough yet — when I delude myself that I can power through and it will all be perfect, I stop, and remember those crabs in the basket in the form of guilty thoughts and disempowering beliefs, using their pinchy sharp claws to keep me from a life of freedom and joy.

If I can't care for me, how can I care for others? So, it seems logical that to care for myself is the most helpful, altruistic, unselfish, generous thing I can do for the people I love and want to serve.

In cutting loose my guilt, how then do I let go of the fear of judgement for courageously dropping those balls and saying "no?" This is one of those journeys that happens fastest and most effectively with a guide like a therapist, life coach, or transformational group work for a permanent shift. To start small, practice exposing yourself to mild embarrassment, make some mistakes and notice how your love-ability and worthiness are not diminished by these.

You can study, research, and listen to podcasts on

the pursuit of well-being to be inspired by people who have proven that they are actually helping the world by helping themselves. Share with others how committing to something small (like putting away all tasks at 8 PM no matter what) has improved your teaching and life. You DO NOT need to explain yourself or make excuses for why you're leaving on time and limiting extra tasks. Instead, allow people to watch you breathe a little easier, walk a little slower, and smile a little more as you make the shift. When it comes to your reasons for setting courageous boundaries, you don't own anyone an explanation. Your contentment is all the explanation anyone needs.

Laying down the guilt of saying "no" gives us the emotional space to thrive. Whether new to teaching or well seasoned, it allows teachers to set aside time to be healthy, happy, and enjoy life with the people we love. And that's what I wish for you. A guilt free practice of setting boundaries, saying "no," and having fun so that you can shine through as the very best version of you and enjoy the beautiful life of love and joy that you deserve. May you enjoy a career in education where you can lounge in the luxury of peeing anytime you want! I know that I never plan to neglect my body in such a barbaric way again. I hope to bump into you in the bathroom line soon, friend!

AFTERWORD

While writing this book the whole world shifted. The Corona virus became a global pandemic that shut the world down and closed schools across the globe. Parents learned a little about what it's like to teach a child and developed a new appreciation for what teachers do. Teachers showed their incredible flexibility and resourcefulness; getting online classrooms up and running and making the shift to a "Maslow before Bloom's" approach to education where relationships and basic needs are met before we ask students to dive into new math concepts.

Then, the brutal murder of George Floyd was filmed and witnessed by the world and launched a giant leap forward in the Black Lives Matter movement against racism and inequity. I shifted immensely in my understanding of the privileged lens that I look through as a white American woman. I see how some of the bold steps I took in my career, while courageous for me, could be downright dangerous for a Black Indigenous Person of Color (BIPOC). I'm grateful to witness and participate in this global awakening and the growing pains that will lead to great change.

Through all of this I celebrated the second year anniversary of Kickass Teacher and I'm three years into my shift from classroom teacher to providing overwhelm support for educators. I'm kicking and screaming for leaders to include realistic, relevant, and empowering well-being strategies in every newsletter, staff training, and meeting. I'm urging them to blend the well-being of teachers into the culture of their schools and to make it the philosophical platform they stand on when leading very emotionally exhausted and stressed out staff.

This book is being written at an incredible time in human history. I feel like it's the first time in 20 years that people are ready to hear what I have to say because so many have decided that excuses like "That's just the way it is," don't cut it anymore. Societies are learning, shifting, and growing at a painful pace thanks to those willing to shout, care, create, march and educate the world. I know that through all of the sickness, violence, and anger, a better society will emerge — one of beauty, compassion and love.

THANKS YOU'S GRATITUDES & BLESSINGS

Anything is possible when you have the right people there to support you.
—MISTY COPELAND

Well...there ya go. The whole crappy book.

I'm so excited to write this section where I get to thank the people waving my flag for more "time to pee." I'm, of course, crying straight through this part.

Let's start with my dad, Mike Johnson. When I was in middle school and struggling to find a research topic for my report, Dad would always have the most interesting people and topics to study. He would spin a tale of the life and intrigues involved in J. Edgar Hoover's FBI, the catastrophe and heartbreak at Hiroshima, or the dark mysteries and secrets of Nostradamus. I'd get so excited to dig into the stories within the hefty book he handed me for my research only to discover that his intriguing mystery or action adventure was buried deep within a boring old textbook. He has a gift for finding the human-ness and intrigue within the drawn-out ledger history can become.

In his late 50's, Dad went to college for the first time and graduated with the Outstanding Academic Achievement Award for his AA degree, and A+++ in his Harvard writing class. I don't think he has missed a single point on a paper or test in his whole college career to date. This led to discovering his extraordinary talent and deep love of writing. He has edited award winning screenplays and narratives. I've told him that he should rewrite text books so we can all be drawn in by the fascinating characters and life that he discovers in every line of dry text. And now, he has done that very thing for my book. No one knows my voice or my heart better and so he has been the perfect person to guide me on this writing journey. When I forgot my voice, he helped me bring it back to the surface loud and clear. Thanks so much for believing in my dream and holding my hand the whole way there, Dad!

Next, I would like to thank one of my very first English professors at Wenatchee Valley College, the very talented author and purveyor of literary insight, Jack Johnson. I came to Jack twenty years after having been his student with a wild idea, "I want to write a book. You wanna be my teacher?" Jack didn't bat an eye. He encouraged me from the very start. I desperately needed someone to keep me on track with deadlines and those darn rules of writing. Jack helped me set up an independent study for an actual grade to write this book. I knew that if grades were on the line, I would get my work done! Jack has just finished publishing his own book of poetry, *The Way We Came In,* and was the perfect guide to walk me through this journey. Even when COVID interrupted our chances to meet in person, he found a way to work with me and keep the ball rolling. I'm deeply grateful that he believed in this dream and was there to support me along the way.

I'm profoundly grateful to my Mom, Julie Johnson, for teaching me to dream big and play hard. She ALWAYS believes in my dreams. Even when my dreams took me into despair, poverty, and heartbreak, she didn't let worry stop her from believing that I had what it took to wade through all of that and come out with my dreams realized. Thanks for giving me my wings, Mom.

My sister, Kathleen Johnson, has been there for so many middle of the night calls when I was feeling stuck and frustrated. God blessed me with the exact sister I asked my parents for when I was two years old. She has been a blessing and miracle as a sister in every way imaginable and is one of the most kick-ass teachers I know. She's out there waving the flag to empower science educators while working as one of the few women scientists with NASA (I know ... she's amazing). She has also waved a flag for every dream I've ever had and I'm grateful for the input and insight she added to this book. As I write this, she is sitting next to me crocheting my birthday present and celebrating every tiny accomplishment as I wade through hours of commas my wonderful father meticulously left for me to add in or take away. Kathleen, thank you for listening to me talk to myself constantly during my final edits without going crazy and for celebrating all of the minor success straight through to this final push.

I have a very long list of beta readers that I'm thrilled to thank. I'm blessed with a group of forty-three incredible educators from around the world who dedicated time to helping me develop my theme and keep the empowerment factor of this book super high. There is no way to describe how uplifting and encouraging it is to have strangers come together to help me kick and scream for teachers. Along with their feedback and insight, they gifted me with beautiful and painful heartfelt stories. These are courageous dedicated professionals who have been a blessing to me and to the world of education. I don't have permission to name everyone and I want those not named to know their support is forever written on my heart.

Thank you to:

Crystal Machado	Emily Rae	Claudette Povey
Heather Holman	Masha Marianna	Jess Mahoney
Julie Heroux Wysocky	Freydlin	Julie Morin
Dawn Hamilton	Melanie Ford	Kellie Herndon
Kimberly Joy Bouch	Emily Grizzell	Pearl Schramm
Lauren N.	Heather Adamson	Marie Andrews
Kari Harder DeMarco	Roxanne Stofbergen	Dacia Myhre
Melissa Rodriguez	Crystal Dickens	Katrina Marie
Dani Crossey	Betsy Kling	Deeann Graham

I also want to thank my fellow Seattle Life Coach Training alumni, Chris Nelson, and Deeann Graham as well as my brilliant friend Crystal Machado for sharing research, resources, time, and advice to help me move forward with this dream.

Can you believe this list keeps going? This is amazing! I have a whole list of my Pre-Sale Super Heroes who dedicated their social media space to spreading the word about this book to all of the teachers they know. They helped me decide on mockups for advertising and sent tons of support my way, waving that flag of encouragement.

Thank you to:

Kathleen Johnson	Deeann Callis Graham	Ayako Nozawa
Ferg Johnson	Ivana Siska Geiger	Lauren Mundinger
Julie Johnson	Summer Rose	Josh Radosevich
Tim Wilbur	Donna Young	Jenn August
Christina Eileen	Malia Reiling	
Heather Rider	Sarah Morgan Hunter	

I never would have learned these valuable lessons without the wonderful connections and life experiences brought to me by my colleagues and students over the years. I want to thank them for all the wonderful laughter; that is one of the biggest blessing brought into my life as a teacher.

I want to shout out to the Facebook groups *#Teacher-Problems* and *Encouraging Teachers* for helping me decide on a book cover. I received over ten-thousand responses and less than ten of them were negative! What a beautiful thing that thousands of perfect strangers across the world will take a minute to give you some love and thumbs up — truly beautiful.

I know this one may seem unusual but I want to send some love to the naysayers who hated my title and questioned my integrity and reasons for writing this book. Even the most cruel feedback had a nugget of treasure hidden within that helped me make my message that much clearer.

Finally, I want to thank the love of my life, Dan Brenner. The man who met me right in the middle of some big dreams. Dan is the kind of guy who made a point of being the very first one to buy a copy of my book and he showed me how to deeply embrace my truest self without fear of what the outside world has to say. Thank you my love.

REFERENCES AND RECOMMENDED READING

Brown, B. (2015). Daring Greatly: How the Courage to be Vulnerable Transforms the Way We Live, Love, Parent, and Lead. New York, NY: Penguin Books.

Brown, B., Dr., & Doyle, G. (2020, March 23). Unlocking Us: [Audio blog post]. Retrieved from https://podcasts.apple.com/us/podcast/unlocking-us-with-bren%C3%A9-brown/id1494350511?i=1000469313957

Chelsom, P. (Director). (2001). Serendipity [Motion picture on DVD]. United States: Buena Vista International.

Cikanavicius, D. (2020). 5 Reasons Why People Stay Silent About Being Abused. Psych Central. Retrieved on July 15, 2020, from https://blogs.psychcentral.com/psychology-self/2019/11/silent-about-abuse/

Dalton-Smith, S. (2019). Sacred rest: Recover your life, renew your energy, restore your sanity. New York, NY: Faith Words.

Kendi, I. X. (2019). How to be an antiracist. New York, NY: One World.

Morten Birkeland Nielsen & Ståle Einarsen (2012) Outcomes of exposure to workplace bullying: A meta-analytic review, Work & Stress, 26:4, 309-332, DOI: 10.1080/02678373.2012.734709

Pink, Daniel H. (2012) Drive: the Surprising Truth about What Motivates Us. New York, NY: Riverhead Books.

Santoro, Doris A. (2018) Demoralized: Why

Teachers Leave the Profession They Love and How They Can Stay. Cambridge, MA: Harvard Education Press.

Surkovich, L. (2020). How and Why Veteran Teachers Persevere: A Phenomenological Study (Unpublished doctoral dissertation). Indiana University of Pennsylvania, Pennsylvania

Twist, L., & Barker T. (2003) The soul of money: transforming your relationship with money and life. New York: Norton.

PRAISE FOR AUTHOR

It's refreshing to know that many of us feel the same way - so much so that an entire book has been compiled to remind us that we are indeed worth more than the piles on our desks. Not only that, but this was all compiled with the feedback and ideas presented from a group of teachers from all different strengths and areas of expertise.

- BETSY KLING, SPECIAL EDUCATION TEACHER

Finally, someone who gets the mental, emotional, and physical drain that is teaching and instead of starting out telling me what I need to do to be better, Jamie is telling me to take care of ME!

- MYREE CONWAY, EARLY EDUCATION TEACHER

I had many dreams when I became a teacher. I knew

that sacrifices would be made; I just didn't think it would be finding the time to go to the bathroom. This book helped me find time to have a life. It helped me bring out the best in me for others and myself to enjoy.

- KIMBERLY BOUCH, MIDDLE SCHOOL TEACHER

I am enough! I am good at what I do! I make a difference! Jamie gave me the permission and validation I need to believe I do enough, even though I cannot do it all!

- JULIE WYSOCKY, ELEMENTARY SCHOOL TEACHER

Kaleigh Killian, High School TeacherJamie J has fantastic ideas on how to keep teachers (and others) sane, happy, and healthy. This book reminds us that we are important as PEOPLE, not just as educators, and she reminds us to celebrate our successes every day.

- KALEIGH KILLIAN, HIGH SCHOOL TEACHER

ABOUT THE AUTHOR

JAMIE JOHNSON

Teacher, author, and transformational life coach, Jamie Johnson, has spent her life exploring and learning how to teach without sacrificing a high quality of life.

Most of her 20 years of teaching were in bilingual elementary classrooms. She has done everything from serving with the Peace Corps in Indonesia to developing an alternative distance learning program in the rural US.

Most recently, Jamie has founded KickassTeacher.com where she serves as an overwhelm support coach for educators seeking a path to fulfill their true calling.